# From Burnout to Bliss

*My Mindful Map*

# EILIS O'GRADY, MSC

All rights reserved. © 2025 Eilis O Grady

978-1-915502-99-5

All intellectual property rights including copyright, design right and publishing rights rest with the author. No part of this book may be reproduced or transmitted in any way including any written, electronic, recording, or photocopying without written permission of the author.

This publication is a personal memoir from the author and views expressed are her own. Insights also shared from her training and expertise in mindfulness.

Published in Ireland by Orla Kelly Publishing.

27 Kilbrody,
Mount Oval,
Rochestown,
Cork,
Ireland.

# DEDICATION

To Mam and Dad - thank you for giving me this life; this wonderful life of exploring what it is to be this human being.

# Contents

**DEDICATION** ............................................................................. xi

**ORIENTATION – Mindfulness as a Map** .......................... xiii

    Current Location ............................................................. xiv

    Your Guide ....................................................................... xv

    The Destination ............................................................. xvii

**CHAPTER 1 – Ways to Awareness** ........................................ 1

    The Starting Point (on the journey to finding the real me)… ....................................................................................... 1

    Mindfulness ......................................................................... 5

    Paying attention ................................................................. 8

    Establishing a Steady Resting Point .............................. 12

    Body Scan ......................................................................... 15

    Sitting Meditation ............................................................ 16

    Mindful Movement .......................................................... 18

    Journaling ......................................................................... 20

Life Coaching ................................................................. 21

📖 Story-time…Distraction ............................................ 22

✒ Pause, Breathe, Reflect .............................................. 24

## CHAPTER 2 – The Guide Posts .................................. 25

Perspective and Programming ..................................... 25

Foundations of Mindfulness ........................................ 29

Gratitude ..................................................................... 29

Generosity ................................................................... 31

Non-Judgement ........................................................... 32

Non-Striving ............................................................... 34

Non-Attachment .......................................................... 35

Patience ....................................................................... 37

Trust, Beginner's Mind, and Letting Go ..................... 38

📖 Storytime…"Maybe" ............................................... 42

✒ Pause, Breathe, Reflect .............................................. 43

## CHAPTER 3 – Practicing the Pause ........................... 44

Pleasure and Power of Being Present ......................... 44

De-blobbing Experience ............................................. 47

Practicing the Pause ............................................................. 49

Creating Balance .................................................................. 51

Human Being ....................................................................... 55

Continuous Manufacturing .................................................. 58

Niksen .................................................................................. 60

📖 Storytime…The Business Man and Fisherman .... 62

🖋 Pause, Breathe, Reflect ............................................ 64

**CHAPTER 4 – Being in the Body** .......................................... 65

Our Relationship With Our Bodies ...................................... 65

Fight, Flight, Freeze ............................................................. 70

Processing Emotions Through the Body ............................ 72

"Turn off the Immersion!" - switching off the stress response ................................................................................ 74

Walking Meditation .............................................................. 77

Afraid of Feeling .................................................................. 78

📖 Storytime… The Felt Sense Prayer ....................... 80

🖋 Pause, Breathe, Reflect ............................................ 83

**CHAPTER 5 - Keep Kind in Mind** .................................................. **84**

    Self-Talk .................................................................................. 84

    Bring Compassion to Suffering ............................................ 90

    Loving Kindness Meditation Practice .................................. 95

    Reactions to Road Blocks ..................................................... 97

    Consuming Social Media, News and TV ............................ 99

    Our words matter ................................................................ 102

    A Mindful Approach to Media Driven Ideals ................... 103

    Storytime… Dragons and Princesses ................................ 106

    Pause, Breathe, Reflect ...................................................... 107

**CHAPTER 6 – Compassion and Companions** ........................... **108**

    In Communication with Others ......................................... 108

    Healthy relationships .......................................................... 113

    Gossip .................................................................................. 114

    Making Connections .......................................................... 116

    Producing Positive Energy ................................................ 118

    Starting a Peace Pandemic ................................................. 121

    Storytime… The World as Our Reflection ......... 125

    Pause, Breathe, Reflect ............................................. 126

## CHAPTER 7 – It's all up to you! ...................................................... 127

Taking Responsibility ................................................... 127

Mountain Meditation .................................................... 130

Letting Go of Expectations of Others ........................... 131

Already Complete ......................................................... 134

Flying Solo .................................................................... 138

Being at Home in Myself .............................................. 141

Ticking the boxes .......................................................... 143

Mind Yourself ............................................................... 145

    Storytime… Copying from Copies ..................... 148

    Pause, Breathe, Reflect ........................................ 149

## CHAPTER 8 – The Journey Ahead ................................................. 150

If in doubt, meditate… .................................................. 150

"Your One Wild and Precious Life" ............................. 152

    Finding the Path of Passions and Purpose ................... 155

    Prioritise and Pursue – No Excuses ............................. 159

    There is nothing to be feared, only understood............ 162

    Time for a Change? ..................................................... 166

    📖 Storytime…The Golden Buddha In You ............. 168

    ✒ Pause, Breathe, Reflect ......................................... 169

**CHAPTER 9 – Buen Camino!** ...................................................... 170

    Some Essentials for the Journey ................................... 170

    Living Life ..................................................................... 171

    Choice and Change ....................................................... 172

    Difficult Emotions ......................................................... 172

    Physical .......................................................................... 174

**A Note on the MBSR** ...................................................... 178

**Working with me** ............................................................ 180

**Bibliography** ................................................................... 181

**Acknowledgements** ......................................................... 182

# ORIENTATION – MINDFULNESS AS A MAP

In a world that often feels overwhelmingly fast-paced and demanding, finding balance and peace can seem like an elusive dream. But what if the key to a fulfilling life lies in the simple practice of mindfulness? With the lived experiences of Eilís, a former corporate professional turned mindfulness teacher, Eilís's own transformation from a life of stress and burnout to one of health, happiness, and vitality is both inspiring and instructive. Through her Master's in Mindfulness Based Wellbeing and decades of experience, Eilís offers insights and practical tools to help you cultivate ease and balance in your daily life. This book is your invitation to slow down, to breathe, and to truly experience the richness of being alive. If you're ready to transform your life and discover the peace within, come in, take a seat, and allow Eilís to guide you on this empowering journey.

As we get started on this transformative journey together, first take a moment to reflect on what is currently happening in your life.

## Current Location

- Do you find yourself living under a constant cloud of stress?
- Does it feel like you're always on the move, rushing from one task to another?
- Are you balancing numerous roles and responsibilities, yet rarely feeling truly fulfilled?
- Is your life a series of deadlines, with little time to breathe in between?
- Do you find solace in comfort food or a drink at the end of the day, only to restart the cycle the next morning?
- Do those Sunday nights fill you with dread for the week ahead?
- Are mornings a struggle, pulling yourself out of bed with little motivation?
- Do feelings of tiredness, anxiety, depression, irritability, or exhaustion seem all too familiar?
- Is there a lingering sense that something crucial is missing from your life?
- Why does happiness seem to evade you, even after achieving all the societal "success" markers?
- Does it feel like life is slipping by, leaving you wondering where all the time has gone?

If any of this resonates with you, it's time to pause and reflect. Happiness and fulfilment are within reach when you take a moment to reassess and realign with what truly matters. Eilís can show you how. Let me introduce you…

# From Burnout to Bliss

**Your Guide**

Hello and welcome, my name is Eilís. If you are looking to create more balance, peace, and ease in your life, come in, take a seat and let me help you with that. I am a teacher of the Mindfulness Based Stress Reduction (MBSR) programme, holding a Masters in Mindfulness Based Wellbeing from University College Cork, Ireland along with being a qualified yoga teacher and life coach.

I grew up as a child of the 80's in a typical, rural, Irish community, going through the normal state exams at school, onto college and getting the good pensionable work that afforded me the nice house, the nice car, the full vibrant social life etc. This was what I had believed success was, this is what the years of education had geared me up to attaining, to live a good and happy life… I thought! And yet when I arrived at the promised destination after working so hard, it was like, is that it now? In addition, through my 20+ years of working as a Chartered Accountant in multinational corporate environments, I experienced the negative consequences of struggling to cope with the fast pace, frantic, busy environments with the back-to-back meetings, productivity targets, cost cutting measures and deadlines to manage. Add to that a mix of decades of unprocessed grief and self-inflicted abusive behaviours from not having the skills to process emotions in any way other than to avoid them, and it made for a real melting pot of stress, depression and unhappiness.

Luckily, I was blessed to have had a breakthrough, albeit by way of absolute burnout in my late thirties. It was a painful period, but I have since learned the importance of navigating life on my own terms and cultivating the capacity to manage life's challenges in order to live a healthy, happy and fulfilling life. At 46 years young, I am so happy to say that I am loving life and feeling healthier and more alive than I ever have before. My life has transformed, physically, mentally and emotionally in a relatively short time. I enjoy more balance, less hunching over spreadsheets and more headstands, less merlot and more meditation and less busyness and more…well… being…human <u>being</u>. I find I have more time, energy and creativity for health, hobbies and work and I ensure to create calm and balance every single day.

The main catalyst for this change was mindfulness. Using the practice and principles of mindfulness to make lasting lifestyle changes has turned me and my life around completely. In the past there were times that I just didn't want to go on, struggling to get out of bed, always feeling exhausted and less than. These days I am jumping out of the bed, full of life and excited to see what a new day will bring! Literally living a life that I could only once dream about. These changes have been so profound that I wanted to share. I took on a Masters Degree in Mindfulness Based Wellbeing and combining this with my learnings from my lived experience, I feel I am now well-equipped to help people navigate their own work/life challenges, to achieve their desired goals, and to enjoy more balance, peace and ease in their lives. I am passionate about sharing what I have learned in order to support and encourage others, be that through the classes and programs I run or simply telling my story about changing my life within the guide posts of mindfulness.

## The Destination

If the idea of reaching a destination filled with more health, happiness, fulfilment, and peace appeals to you, then allow me to share my guide for getting there. Discovering mindfulness felt like being handed a manual titled "How to Be a Happy Human." It set me on a path of self-discovery and empowerment, leading to a life enriched with balance and creativity. Mindfulness tools have helped me cultivate more contentment, joy, and freedom, and now, I hope to pass this knowledge onto you through my work.

## This book is part of my work and in it:

- I will be sharing with you some practical tools that you can implement into your life to further your journey towards flourishing in every aspect. These tools are designed to seamlessly integrate into your daily routine, empowering you to make mindful choices that enhance your well-being.
- Additionally, I will be encouraging the cultivation of self-awareness through reflective pieces and carefully crafted exercises that invite introspection and growth.
- As you navigate through these practices, you will encounter stories from my own life, illustrating the real-life application of mindfulness and demonstrating the tremendous impact it has had on my ability to thrive, so you can thrive too.

Remember, no map claims to be the entire territory. I am here to act as your guide, offering support, listening, and walking alongside you as much as I can. We are all companions on this journey, as beautifully captured in the words of Ram Dass: "we are all just walking each other home."

*Eilís O'Grady*
*Mindfulness, Yoga and Life Coaching*
*+353 87 6523410*
*www.eilisogrady.ie*
*www.instagram.com/eilisogrady*
*www.facebook.com/eilis.ogrady*

# CHAPTER 1 – WAYS TO AWARENESS

*"Knowing yourself is the beginning of all wisdom." –*
*Aristotle, Metaphysics (350 BC)*

The first step on this journey is building self-awareness. The invitation is simply to step out of the virtual reality of autopilot, where we are either living in the future or in the past through the vehicle of our minds.

**The Starting Point (on the journey to finding the real me)...**

After another tense and stomach-churning work meeting with my boss at the time, I remember leaving their office, filled with rage and on the verge of crying. This was becoming a more common occurrence as my previously strong exterior began to break down from years of being overstretched. My once super-powered ability to internalise the associated feelings of such intense situations was becoming weaker and externally, signs were beginning to show. I was reaching my limits of avoiding and suppressing long held emotions. For some reason, I decided this time was going to be different, and uncharacteristically I walked to my desk, picked up my handbag and left the building. I went to the doctor downtown, who diagnosed me with stress related vertigo and prescribed me a couple of weeks off work.

In hindsight, I see different aspects at play here and I can only speak to the probable underlying causes on my own side. Firstly, I never felt good enough, in any aspect of my life, so I relied on external approval for my sense of self-worth. I strived to be perfect for fear of criticism. My reputation for being a 'good worker' was an identity I attached firmly to. I interpreted negative work feedback as a failure and a direct personal attack as opposed to an opportunity for development. Even mild feedback would feel threatening to me because I had no sense of inner belief or self-confidence. I relied solely on others' positive assessments of me to feel good in myself. The physical symptoms apparent on that day when I left work were a testament to the fact that I felt so threatened that I literally ran away.

I also see now that I never really loved accounting. Yes, I was good at organising, structuring, presenting pretty PowerPoints and Excel spreadsheets but numbers… no, definitely not, average at very best! All through the process of choosing subjects in secondary school, the love for subjects was never an important consideration. Like most others, the priority was, where was I going to get the most points to get a college course that would lead me to getting the best paid job possible. And I understand completely why this was the decision process at the time. Most parents and teachers of that generation had grown up in an Ireland that had seen very lean times and had likely experienced and/or witnessed scarcity of basic needs over their younger lives. The fear of another possible recession taking them back to where there would be a lack again was a very real threat in their minds and they were doing their best to guide their young people towards recession proof careers.

    I worked as a Chartered Accountant for over 20 years after qualifying, mainly in the Pharmaceutical/Medical Device industry, always meeting my performance targets and I would say, fairly well respected for my work. Like anyone else in the industry, I experienced the pressures, demands and stresses that these dynamic and fast-moving working environments can bring to an employee's life. However, this was being added to the pile of unprocessed emotions already accumulated in my body from (1) the grief of my Dad's passing at a young age, (2) the traumatic circumstances surrounding his death that night, (3) and the trauma from my own self-hatred since early teens, all of which I will speak more about later. Lacking the necessary life skills and tools at the time to deal with any of it, the subsequent negative consequences on health and relationships were becoming more and more evident. As the years went on, the cracks in the protective armour that I had built around me were beginning to show. The over-eating, over-drinking, and over-working in an effort to deal with the accumulating stress and difficult emotions were beginning to cause more downstream issues. I lived for weekends, only to pack them with people pleasing social activities to make up for the guilt of not being able to catch up with friends/family during the week, which left me feeling even more exhausted. When I finally got to my annual summer break or Christmas holidays, I was wrecked and often became ill from running on adrenaline during the year! It was a never-ending cycle of stress, illness and internal unhappiness.

## Eilis O'Grady

During my sick leave from work, I was so desperate for a change that I contemplated leaving the job. I remembered how I loved my part time pub work during college so, as a lovely lady publican in Dungarvan will attest to, I got a trial run for a few nights. She offered me a job but I had quickly realised during the three night trial, that although I loved pulling pints and interacting with customers, the sleep deprivation from the after-hours clean-up was not sustainable for me. (I always smile when I remember that trial period ☺). I contemplated farming – maybe that was the answer! I was reared on it, could drive a tractor from a young age, and I could even shear sheep. I had completed the "Green Cert." (Level 6 Advanced Certificate in Agriculture – FETAC) with Kildalton College a few years prior. So I hung out with my uncle Tom during my time off too and seriously considered the possibility. In the end, I held off, parked my ideas and instead took myself to a counsellor first.

Sitting in a small room at a local health clinic talking to the counsellor, I was explaining how I had depression, I was on medication (albeit a small dose) and that this was something that I inherited, "it was in the family". At that time, I was resigned to having it for the rest of my life. This was my narrative, my story and a "fact" of my life as part of living in the box that I had put myself in. I had assigned various labels to myself within my box such as "good girl", "diligent", "hard working", "prone to depression", "accountant", "been through a lot", "unattractive", "ugly", "fat", "average" and this would form my identity for life. The labels were a mix of terms from early school reports, phrases that I had received from authority figures and some of my own. Although I cannot recall the counsellor's exact response, I remember wondering why he isn't feeling sorry for me? Why isn't he agreeing with me? Does he not believe me? But I have a diagnosed clinical problem! I remember being quite put out and insulted by his response (or lack thereof) and thinking "how dare he, he has no idea". I felt that he had offended, not just me but, my family too, as this is what was accepted as a valid reason at home when I felt low. Of course, the "good" girl that I was wouldn't utter a word in refute to the man, such a respected authority figure, but kept all these thoughts running around inside. Looking back, this was the painful junction... this was the moment when someone questioned, even dismissed, my narrative. My story of victimhood and my world view was thrown into mid-air! This was the starting point.

## Mindfulness

I sat stunned and shaken yet I listened just enough in the aftermath of his unsympathetic response to absorb two words that would ultimately go on to change my life... "neuroplasticity" and "mindfulness". He introduced the notion that the brain can be trained and does not necessarily take on a fixed mode of operation for one's entire life. This was a groundbreaking notion for me. I had thought you were born in a certain way and that was your fate; a leopard doesn't change his spots and all that... (I despise this saying now). He advised me to look into taking a mindfulness course, which I had never heard of, and the rest, as they say, is history. Although very sceptical, there was obviously just enough curiosity (and/or desperation) in me to investigate this empowering notion of neuroplasticity. Neuroplasticity, also known as brain plasticity, is the remarkable ability of the brain to change and adapt to new experiences by forming new neural connections throughout life. Through the help of MRI scanning technology, mindfulness meditation is proven to promote structural changes in the brain that enhance emotional regulation and stress management. The idea of being able to rewire our brains meant that there may be a way out of the box of depression!

So after the counselling, I soon enrolled in an 8-week Mindfulness Based Cognitive Therapy (MBCT) course, which was developed from the Mindfulness Based Stress Reduction (MBSR) course, the original Mindfulness Based Program. Both courses are quite similar with slightly different emphasis. MBCT has been shown to be effective in reducing the risk of relapse in individuals who have experienced recurrent episodes of depression, while MBSR is more directly targeted at reducing stress. This course was the first step in taking my power back and taking responsibility for my life. The first step away from being a victim and breaking open the self-created boxes that I was living within. Even entering into counselling, I suspect I was really looking for someone to feel sorry for me, validate my story and maybe alleviate my pain for me in that way. Mindfulness is different. In short, it's not therapy, it's more like a tool to help someone help themselves and address their unique set of life circumstances at any time in life. It helps find a way of being in the world that reduces suffering and creates more calm and ease within chaotic situations. Mindfulness is not about sitting in the lotus position on top of a secluded mountain or even about relaxation (although it may be a positive consequence of the practice). It is also important to note that mindfulness is not a religion. It is a secular practice that has been widely adopted in fields such as education, healthcare, and corporate settings, where it is valued for its ability to improve focus, emotional regulation, and mental clarity without requiring adherence to a particular faith.

Research over the past 45 years has proven time and time again that mindfulness works for the majority of people who engage with it in terms of lowering reoccurrence of depression and reducing anxiety along with many other benefits. Studies have even shown that it can be as effective as anti-depressant medication, which I am a testament to myself but yet which I would not (nor advise anyone to) substitute under any circumstances without consulting a doctor first. It encompasses learning the skill of paying attention, which is hugely valuable in a modern society that's experiencing a rapid decline in the capacity due to the advent of technology. Using this capacity to pay attention, we gain more awareness of ourselves and how we are showing up in the world – maybe seeing how old, conditioned behaviours are actually the sources of the stress in our lives. With this new awareness we can make better choices for ourselves and take more mindful actions with the help of the guiderails of the core foundations of mindfulness, which are: non-judging, gratitude, patience, a beginner's mind, trust, non-striving, acceptance, letting go and generosity. (These are explored more in-depth in chapter 2). Through these, it offers a new way of showing up and being in the world.

Learning the basics of mindfulness through an 8-week program and continuing the practice on an ongoing basis in daily life is certainly not a quick fix. It's more akin to going to the gym or adopting a healthy eating plan to attain and maintain a healthy weight; I think of it as a slow accumulation of wisdom. Like a consistent gym goer, the consistent mindfulness practitioner will enjoy lasting benefits including calm, peace and ease even in the midst of the most difficult times. It takes daily practice to build and maintain the muscle of paying attention and the best gym for mindfulness is in fact… a busy mind! Some people discount mindfulness with the statement, "oh my mind is too busy for mindfulness", when in fact, that's exactly the type of mind that mindfulness will benefit most! More thoughts are like more weights to train with! The course invites us to take on an 8 week exploration of what it is to be a human being and how best to navigate the territory to discover a place of peace, ease and contentment. The in-depth curriculum is covered in a 650 page book called "Full Catastrophe Living". Jon Kabat Zinn was moved to write this book on witnessing the transformations in body and mind from his MBSR participants in the stress reduction clinic at the University of Massachusetts Medical Centre in the 1970's. It's interesting to note how it implies living fully within the chaos of life, acknowledging that there will always be challenges in life and the reassurance that we can still be content and fulfilled within these times with practice.

**Paying attention**

The skill of paying attention should not be underrated because in today's society it is becoming an increasingly rare ability. It is said that in the year 2000 the average attention span of an adult was about 12 seconds but over the years, with the introduction of social media and advances in technology, that the average has dropped to 8 seconds. While the average attention span of a goldfish is 9 seconds! Now although the robustness of the scientific support behind these findings is questionable, what is clear is that the constant barrage of information and technology can challenge our ability to focus. So if we want to increase our capacity for self-awareness, then building the brain's ability to focus attention is essential.

Paying attention is a key feature of what we term "human being" as opposed to the more habitual "human doing" mode of modern living that we engage in. Human doing is characterized by operating on autopilot, focusing on tasks and goals, often driven by the need to avoid discomfort. It fixates on thoughts as reality, with a narrow focus on achieving objectives, sometimes to the point of exhaustion. It has a frantic frenzied energy to it. On the other hand, "human being mode" means living with more conscious awareness and intentionality, harvesting wisdom from the body to approach life's challenges and not relying solely on the thinking mind.

It is said that we have between 60,000-90,000 thoughts a day and 90% of them are the same day after day. This is not a big surprise when we begin to take a look at how we spend our day to day lives (which we will do in chapter 7). Aside from the odd break for annual leave perhaps, we often find ourselves repeating the same day over and over again. In and of itself, this is not a problem provided that these days are being lived with a high level of conscious awareness, allowing us to know the uniqueness of moments throughout our days and subsequently experiencing life as full and enriching. However, this is not the case for many, who's days are not only the same in terms of the same routines, commutes, work schedules and habits but also being lived on autopilot mode. This way of life develops into repeating the same months and then years living through thinking, in the virtual realities of the future and the past and bypassing the felt sense of the gift of the present.

Lives can seem unfulfilling and somehow empty, despite the materialistic wealth we have surrounded ourselves with. I often think of Bryan Adam's "Summer of '69" song "those were the best days of our lives" and "that summer seemed to last forever", referring to the richness of life in the younger days. But while there "ain't no use in complainin'", we don't have to give into resignation that our life situations have to remain the same. We can choose differently at any stage in life, at any age. When we develop the capacity to step out of our habitual ways of thinking and behaving, we can start to see that we have more options and choices than we realised. We can go from existing to fully living and savouring the richness and variety of life.

The "raisin exercise" is a mindfulness practice that I take participants through which demonstrates experientially the richness we can cultivate from the smallest simplest things in life when we step out of autopilot and bring conscious awareness to what we are engaged in. Participants are invited to take a raisin and experience it using the full range of senses, sight, touch, smell, taste, even sound! It is something that needs to be experienced but suffice to say that the insights garnered from such a tiny object can be immense. Amongst other discoveries, it can show the benefits of slowing down, bringing a curious mind and coming back to our senses…literally!

Mindfulness practices can represent a microcosm of our lives. They can highlight to us our habitual ways of thinking, reacting and behaving. Each practice invites us to consider how these ways impact on our daily lives and prompt us to question whether these patterns of behaviour are helpful to us in the pursuit of calm, peace and ease in our lives.

> **Exercise – Consider the speed at which you live your life and ask yourself:**
> - What, or more importantly who (including myself), might I be missing in the fast pace of life?
> - What or who else am I not appreciating in my life?
> - Where else could my life taste sweeter if I would just slow down and savour it more often?

## Establishing a Steady Resting Point

Even a few minutes of solitude a day can be so beneficial to check in with your inner self. A few minutes a day where you are just sitting, no other inputs, no screen, no book, no ear pods, nothing. Best having the gaze lowered or eyes closed to take your awareness inwards and simply check in on the internal weather pattern. We can spend so much time concerned by the meteorological external weather and forecasts on the radio, T.V. and our phones but relatively little time tuning into the internal body barometer. Checking in and listening to the body regularly can give a surprisingly accurate indication for brewing internal pressure and stress or other internal weather events, such as mood changes or emotional turmoil.

During any mindfulness practice, the mind will wander because that's what minds do. They go off into thinking about the future or the past, to-do lists, remembering, worrying, planning, etc. This is a very natural part of the process of meditation and provides the training weight for the muscle of mindfulness to be built. At the beginning of each practice, an anchor point is chosen that offers a clear, safe place to focus on and where the attention can be easily directed back to in order to ground awareness into the present moment after the mind has wandered. Bringing the awareness back to this focus point over and over as the mind does its thing is like gently tugging back an untrained puppy.

The anchor is also a home base where the attention can rest during moments of intensity. Maybe when you find your mind has hijacked your attention away from the present and it's busying itself with overthinking, ruminating, resisting, wanting or craving.

Or maybe when the body is experiencing strong sensations, the anchor provides a place of steadiness and calm to resource ourselves when needed. I like to imagine it like experiencing the calm of the deep blue sea, anchor fixed firmly to the sea bed underneath the passing waves of sensations, impulses, thoughts and emotions on the surface of the ocean.

When we can bring ourselves right back to the moment like this, we create a space and moments of awareness from which real wisdom arises and where your full true self resides. The ability to step out of autopilot and revert the mind back from the thoughts of the future or the past and onto whatever it is we are engaged in presently, ensures that we are bringing our whole complete selves into the activity, resulting in more powerful and effective action. Whether it is being fully engaged in a work meeting, lining up a golf shot or playing with your children, the experience can be enriched by being fully in it, as opposed to having your body and mind disconnected…the headless chicken effect.

**Choice of anchors include:**

- The Breath – simply paying attention to the felt sense of the breath in the body; the areas that you feel it most; the pace, texture, rhythm, sound of the breath etc.
- Sensations in the Feet/Seat/Hands – similar to the breath, feeling the sensations of the feet/seat/hands as opposed to thinking about. Noticing contact points, temperature, pressure or internal pulsing, tingling, circulation, aliveness inside etc.
- Sounds – noticing sounds in the environment, up close, in the distance, even internally in the body. Paying attention to the

rhythm, pitch, tone or even the silence between sounds. Not needing to label or create a story or commentary around the sound but more imagining hearing the sound for the very first time.

Inviting a beginner's mind to the experience of whatever anchor is chosen by cultivating a willingness to see, feel and hear things as if for the first time means we drop our preconceived notions of how we think things *should* be and see everything (and maybe everyone) with fresh eyes. Another valuable skill that we can transfer into daily living.

- Standing in a queue, be it in a shop or a bank or whatever, is a great place to practice steading and grounding with an anchor point of choice.
- Toilet breaks are also great opportunities to take mindful moments throughout the day! No matter how busy you are, you just gotta' go! It's at least one time in the day where you are alone for enough time to just take a breath and step out of autopilot!

## Body Scan

The body scan is a meditation practice that is generally taken in a lying down position. Participants are guided to place attention into the various areas of the body as the anchor point for their attention and simply noticing what's present in terms of felt sensations. And when the mind wanders off into mental activity, re-anchoring the awareness back on the part of the body being attended to.

With so many jobs being more mentally demanding than physically so, the body scan can also be a great way to re-balance. In our busy modern worlds, we can live so much in our heads that we can end up completely disconnected from our bodies. During my time working as a financial analyst, it always seemed to be busy with some priority project and before I had the coping skills to manage it, the first thoughts on waking would be what was on the task list for the day. In the shower and getting dressed, I would already be in the morning meetings in my head, preparing what I needed to say and playing out various potential scenarios. The whole day would be rehearsed in my head and I would feel like I had a day's work done before I even entered the building! I had missed the enjoyment of a hot shower, the flavor and aroma of a good cup of coffee and the beautiful sounds of nature on my commute, all from being lost in thought and disconnected from my body. The body scan practice invites us to deliberately set time aside to inhabit the body away from maybe being lost in our heads for large parts of our days (and lives!).

The guidance includes an invitation to bring a kind and caring attitude in our paying of attention to the body. For so many years (decades, in fact), I hated how my body looked (or maybe more accurately, how I perceived how it looked). The relationship I had with my body was toxic and it was little wonder that I never felt good in my own skin. Like so many others, I had bought into the ideals of "the perfect body" within the social media culture, exposed myself to unrealistic edited images and engaged in the poisonous practice of comparison. I judged my body harshly and critically for continuing to come up less than the latest trend and berated it on the daily. When the body scan was introduced to me, the notion of adopting a kind, gentle and caring attitude towards my body was alien. It was very awkward, like bringing together two warring factions to shake hands for the first time. But gradually I began to experience it like a reacquaintance with an old friend, who I hadn't visited in years, and I started to re-build the broken relationship. Eventually finding that my body was becoming a trusted and wise friend to me on my life's journey. After a time, the body scan can feel more like "coming home", and becomes a place of safety, where I can cultivate a sense of steadiness and calm whenever I need it.

**Sitting Meditation**

The sitting meditation practice usually means sitting on a chair or a cushion on the floor maybe, in a tall, alert, yet comfortable position where possible. We anchor our attention onto a chosen focus point like the breath sensations, or the felt sensations of the feet, seat or hands or if for any reason the body is uncomfortable to focus on, sounds are a good place to anchor attention. We will experience the mind wandering off as usual and then the training is to notice it has gone into some mental activity, like planning, remembering, worrying or daydreaming, and gently and kindly inviting the attention back to where it was intended… the breath, body or sounds.

We can learn a lot about the nature of our minds. When I began to sit like this and observe where my mind tended to wander to, I noticed it went into the future and planning more often than not. I was living in the future a lot! So by practicing the bringing back of the attention onto the anchor of my breath usually, I built up the muscle of mindfulness and living in the present moment. Each time I brought my awareness back was like a bicep curl rep for the muscle of the brain and over time the duration of my daydreaming and planning my life away into the future was reduced.

After sitting for a while, particularly as a new meditator, the body will likely become uncomfortable. Often urges to move, scratch an itch or just leave the practice altogether arise. This proves to be a perfect "grist for the mill" in learning how to sit with difficulty and process associated emotions in a healthy way. We learn that any moment, either has a pleasant, an unpleasant, or a neutral feeling tone to it and the mind likes to judge each moment into liking, disliking, right, wrong, good or bad. As we will discover in chapter 2, this is the judging mind and it can create a lot of unnecessary suffering for us if not managed. Sitting practice helps us to understand that each moment, no matter how overwhelming they may seem at times, is just some combination of four elements: (1) sensations (2) impulses (3) thoughts (4) emotions (or SITE as an acronym). Practicing to dissect or "de-blob" moments within this framework proves very useful when working with stress, difficulty and overwhelming times in our lives and we will explore this more as we go on.

## Mindful Movement

I can't recall exactly but I feel my view of yoga growing up was something like "what's the point in doing that! It's too slow to burn calories and lose weight". Everything revolved around my weight issues in those days. In my thirties, I would have taken some sports-oriented classes with the intention of preventing injury and increasing flexibility. It was shortly after I turned forty that I was in a yoga class and thought, "this is so good for me and it might just help keep me out of the old folks home for longer when I get older". I enrolled in a yoga teacher training course in Waterford city with absolutely no intention to teach it but just to learn more about it so that I could have a stronger practice for the longer term. I was finishing up the course when COVID hit. Later that year, my friend Colette proposed that I might run a class in the local community hall as people just needed some activities that could be done outside of lockdowns and within the pandemic restrictions at the time. I laughed at her and said "Not a hope! Who would turn up to a *yoga* class in Modeligo! It would be you, me and maybe my mother!." After a lot of persuasion, I gave in and before I knew it, I was teaching classes in neighbouring communities of Touraneena, Ballymacarbry, Melleray, and Ballinameela too!

The course opened my eyes to what yoga is really all about. It's certainly less about strong warrior poses or standing on your head as I had thought. The word "Yoga" means "to yoke" or "join" or "unite" and when we speak of practicing yoga, it refers to bringing body, mind and spirit into alignment. In having head, heart and gut aligned in whatever we do, we are firing on all cylinders as opposed to just allowing our, often busy, minds to rule our lives. Movement through gentle yoga poses is a form of mindfulness meditation. It's similar to the body scan in terms of building the relationship with the body and I find that it's an ideal method for newcomers to mindfulness. It serves as a bridge over what can be a very big gap between a participant's fast paced life and, say, a sitting still practice. In addition to all the mental health benefits of mindfulness meditation, yoga/mindful movement also builds strength, flexibility and balance in the body, while reducing the risk of injury. It also cultivates a greater body awareness, so that we can be alert to early warning signs of illness or changes within the body.

On an emotional level, it is an effective way to work with and release emotions (i.e. energy in motion) within the body so that this energy doesn't get stuck and cause dis-ease down the road. Yoga, as part of a therapeutic approach, can be very helpful in relieving the suffering of bereavement within the grieving process. The yoga breathing can serve as a powerful way to regulate emotions, through stimulating the autonomic nervous system. Breath-work can bring the system back into balance after the triggering of a stress response (i.e. fight, flight, freeze) in the body and so reducing the health risks associated with chronic stress. Other associated benefits include relaxation, optimal lung function, emotional balance and improved sleep quality.

> Yoga can be practiced by anyone, no matter what their physical capabilities because it is more about the alignment of head, heart and gut in any activity that is being engaged in and less about touching your toes.

The above are the main mindfulness practices to help harness the skill of paying attention. Other meditations with slightly different emphasises will be explored in later chapters: Walking Meditation (chapter 4), Loving Kindness (chapter 5), Mountain Meditation (chapter 7).

## Journaling

Personally, I think, nothing beats yoga and meditation in terms of promoting self-awareness but there are certainly techniques that enhance and support the practices. Journaling is a fantastic resource and can serve multiple purposes. Like mindfulness, it has been shown in scientific research to improve symptoms of anxiety and depression. It is a great addition to a strong morning routine (see chapter 7) and after a night's sleep, I find gathering the thoughts flying around in my head onto a page can help clear the mental clutter and create clarity of mind for the day ahead. I also find it a very helpful way to process big complicated emotionally triggering situations and life events too. Writing down how you are feeling, and thinking, about a situation can be so cathartic. Voice note journaling with the smartphone's voice recorder is something I also find so useful if I'm on a walk or out and about. Just speaking something out loud can not only provide a sense of unburdening but can also bring clarity or a new perspective to something that would otherwise endlessly rattle around in the mind. A "better out than in" approach.

## Life Coaching

Recognising that making positive life changes is so worth it but almost never easy, a life coach guides and encourages clients through personal or career challenges and/or serves as an accountability partner to reach their ultimate goals. Talking to friends/family can be great but they can be biased in their views and counsel. Life coaching is a way to access an independent and non-judgemental sounding board in a safe confidential space, where problems can be explored; structure and clarity put around scattered thoughts or ideas; or where a way forward can be discovered within a project or goal that currently seems stuck. Coaching can change the way we think about things. As mentioned, most of our thoughts are repetitive but when we are asked new questions, we come up with new and creative answers! New thoughts = new results (vs. same daily thoughts = same daily results). Similar to mindfulness, coaching is not advice, therapy, or counselling and is more about creating awareness in ourselves to allow us to respond and make the best possible choices for ourselves in pursuit of a fuller and happier life.

As a brief aside, how I got into becoming a life coach myself was also not as I planned. All I knew was there was a program that some companies were sending managers, and potential managers, on for their development in preparation for career progression. With fresh energy, from the lifeline that the 8-week mindfulness course had provided me, and the intention of accelerating my career in the corporate world after my period of burnout, I applied for the training. I had the encouragement and kind support of my management at the time (thank you Kieran and Michael) to take the course which I really appreciated. But I remember sitting in the first of the classes in late 2018 and silently thinking "this is fluff", "this must be a con", "so you're telling me that I can help people *without* giving them my advice! That the process is less about *telling* people what to do and more about providing space to really *listen* to people!!" Clearly I had a lot to learn but my childhood school ways came through and I did learn diligently and quickly. The truth is that each unique individual is the expert of themselves. No therapist, coach, priest, manager or any other authority figure can give you better advice than your own inner wisdom. The best that they can do is be a catalyst for your self-awareness out of which this wisdom emerges.

 **Story-time…Distraction**

The following piece illustrates the importance of mindfulness and being able to pay attention. It also highlights how busyness is so frequently unproductive, exhausting and often used as a strategy for procrastination and avoidance:

I decided to hose the garden, as I turn on the hose in my driveway, I look at my car and decide it needs washing.

As I start towards the garage, I notice the mail on the porch table that I brought up from the mailbox earlier. I decide to go through the mail before I wash the car.

I lay down my car keys on the table, put the junk mail in the rubbish bin underneath the table and notice the bin is full, so I decided to put the bills back on the table and take out the rubbish first but then I think I am going to be near the mailbox when I am putting out the rubbish anyway so I may as well pay the bills.

I take out my cheque book and notice that there is only one cheque left. My extra cheques are in the study so I go inside, where I find the can of coke that I had been drinking…. I need to push the can of coke aside so that I don't accidentally knock it over. The coke is getting warm so I decide to put it in the fridge.

As I head towards the kitchen with the coke, the vase of flowers on the kitchen counter catches my eye and I notice they need water…. It actually goes on….

And at the end of the day, the car isn't washed, the bills aren't paid, there is a warm can of coke sitting on the counter, the flowers still don't have enough water, there is still only one cheque in my cheque book and now I can't find the remote for the TV.

When I try to find out why I've gotten nothing done today, I am really baffled because I know that I was really busy and I am really tired.

I realise this is a serious problem and need to get help but first I must check my email.

**Pause, Breathe, Reflect**

- What have you been doing today that could be referred to as "autopilot", where your mind was thinking of something other than what you were physically engaged in?
- How often do you check the internal weather patterns of the body, heart and mind relative to the meteorological weather forecasts on TV, radio or your phone?
- Would you describe your relationship with your body as a friendship, a passing acquaintance or a foe?

# CHAPTER 2 – THE GUIDE POSTS

*"Change the way you look at things, and the things you look at change." – Wayne Dyer*

How we interpret situations creates our reality and the foundations of mindfulness offers us a new way of perceiving life.

**Perspective and Programming**

During childhood we depend on our caregivers for survival and naturally learn ways of being and behaving that will secure the love and attention from them accordingly. For the most part, it would be hoped that these instructions from parents, teachers etc. were for our own safety. However often they may have spilled over into being motivated by the fulfilment of the needs of the authority figure or framed in such a way that we learned to betray our own wants to please them. Staying quiet, not drawing attention to yourself, being a good girl, eating up all your dinner (hungry or not), do what the teacher says, never question your parents/ priests, and conforming to standard norms were the generally accepted rules, of my time at least, to secure attention, approval and survival.

In early life we seemed to adapt quite logically to the environments we found ourselves in and took on behaviours and habits to garner what we needed. It was important that we did as we depended on these people for our lives. As we grow into independent adults, our needs change but we either don't have the time or are not aware that we are still carrying outdated ways of being. We continue to be the obedient conscientious employee, saying yes to all requests while ignoring our physical limits to the detriment of our health. We carry on people pleasing to obtain external approval while betraying our own needs, wants and desires. Or striving to keep up with fashion trends to fit in and conform but meanwhile suppressing the true and full expression of ourselves. These are all just examples of self-protection behaviours that we build up around ourselves that become our belief systems. They disconnect us and create distance from our true and authentic essence, which by the time we land into adulthood we have forgotten. From years of putting the needs of others first, we generally don't consider whether our ways of being are helping or hindering us towards the attainment of what we need as an adult. Our changing needs and the ever changing circumstances we find ourselves can simply go unexamined in the busyness of life. Without introspection we can continue to seek the approval and external validation of others to fulfil our needs and to feel a momentary sense of self-worth. (Just like the immense self-esteem you felt if you answered a question really well for the "religious inspector" in primary school in front of the classroom… yes, a "religious inspector"…an absolutely bonkers concept but a reality that would fill your little body with the fear of God in the 80's!!)

But now is the time for re-claiming our own power...

In chapter 1 we looked at coming back to our senses, quite literally. We slow down to connect with the bodily functions of touching, tasting, smelling, hearing and seeing. We build on this now to investigate how we make sense of the various sensory inputs from the world. I liken the brain to a central processing unit (CPU) of a computer, where raw data is inputted, then the CPU applies various algorithms and formulas to come up with a result. In the same way the brain takes in the data through the senses and applies various perceptions and interpretations, which result in our unique individual version of reality.

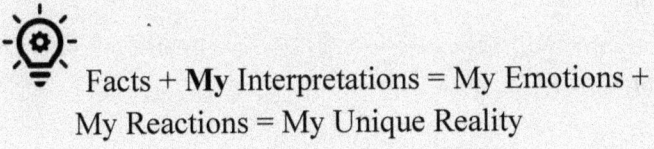

Facts + **My** Interpretations = My Emotions + My Reactions = My Unique Reality

Our perceptions and interpretations are based on our own past experience and include beliefs, cultural influences, education, attitudes, assumptions, unconscious bias, associations, attachments and preferences. Much of what we "experience" is actually memory. It's a processing shortcut our brain uses to reduce processing energy and time. Along with these, our mood, hormones and energy at the time of processing an event can have a major impact on the resulting reality, which creates our emotions and reactions to the, otherwise neutral, event. Usually this process is instant and happens so quickly that we don't get time to question it but if we can slow down and create enough of a pause to ask ourselves questions like the following, we might be able to see that we have much choice and control over "our reality".

> **Exercise – Calling to mind a recent challenging situation, ask yourself:**
> - how am I processing this event?
> - what old beliefs might I be applying here that are no longer relevant or useful?
> - what meaning am I giving to this?
> - who's expectations am I applying?
> - what assumptions and judgements am I taking into this scenario?
>
>    (Assumptions are unreliable at best and can be very damaging – be sure to question them!)

We begin to notice that our minds play a significant part in creating our reality, emotions and reactions. We can choose to interrupt old ways of processing to arrive at new realities, new views and new ways of relating to the world. It's much like de-commissioning the old software and programming in the new updated versions. We can often live within the narrow remits of our virtual realities created by our past experiences, present mood states and predictions around the future and our worlds can get very confined and suffocating. The challenge is to stand back and take a wider view of situations to allow us to see more options in terms of how we might perceive a situation. Bringing ourselves back into the expansive open living space of our bodies anchors our awareness and provides this perspective, which can bring more choice, freedom and ease. The power of one new thought can not only transform an experience but it can be absolutely life changing from that point forward!

## Foundations of Mindfulness

Taking more mindful actions with the help of the guide-rails of the core foundations of mindfulness was mentioned in the previous chapter and these foundations also provide a selection of new lenses from which to view and approach life events. Not only does the practice of mindfulness strengthen our skills in paying attention and gaining awareness of how we show up in the world, it also offers us new ways of processing our experiences and ways of being that may be more conducive to our health and wellbeing. We first become aware of our conditioned beliefs and habitual tendencies, many of which can cause us stress and suffering and then we learn how to approach life through the mindfulness attitudes of non-judging, patience, a beginner's mind, trust, non-striving, acceptance, letting go, generosity and gratitude. From personal experience, I can say that this way of living has brought so much more ease to living, a whole new way of being with myself and others and best of all, opportunities and life experiences that I couldn't even have dreamt of previously!

## Gratitude

Nowadays, I wake up every morning and gratitude is my first thought... be that for the lovely sleep I've had or the sun shining in the window or simply the aliveness and health in my body. This was a skill that I trained myself into and is a drastic change to what my mornings used to be. I went through years of waking up with so much fear, dread and anxiety running through my veins, wondering how I was going to get out of the bed, never mind how I was going to get through the day. There was often guilt and shame for the binge eating and/or drinking that I had engaged in the night before on top of the physical unease in my stomach. It was very dark at times, yet today, it's almost unfathomable that I went through all that. Life can change relatively quickly once you set your intention to it.

In the early days, I started off with writing down 3 things I was grateful for every morning; little things, anything. My guide to people is to be grateful for having running water and everything else is a bonus. As with any new habit, it felt very strange and unnatural at first, but it is a groundbreaking practice that creates an abundant mindset. I've changed methods several times from gratitude journaling to a gratitude jar on the kitchen counter to a gratitude sheet held with a magnet on the fridge to simply regularly calling to mind all that I am grateful for, but it continues to be a daily practice no matter what the method. Intentionally setting my first thought of the day to one of gratitude and, as best I can, remembering to say "thank you" before closing my eyes to sleep at night are key ingredients for the peaceful and abundant life I now enjoy. Current research backs this up and highlights several benefits of maintaining a gratitude practice, encompassing psychological, physical, and social aspects. A gratitude practice has been found to reduce symptoms of depression and anxiety, lower blood pressure, improve sleep quality and enhance relationships.

> 💡 The Gratitude Jar - each day write down one thing for which you're grateful on a post-it note/small piece of paper, fold it and put it into a clear glass jar. Maybe place on the kitchen countertop where they collect as a visual reminder of the good things in your world. (This is a nice one to involve kids in too!). It's also a lovely end of the year ritual to take time to open the jar and the notes to remind yourself of all the abundance in your life.

## Generosity

Closely linked with an abundant mindset is generosity. When I think of the term "generosity", my mind immediately jumps to charitable donations or volunteering. Of course, it's a much wider construct and can incorporate giving time, energy and attention to others. Mindful listening in interacting with others is possibly the greatest gift that you can give someone. This is the giving of not only your time but your full attention, without judgement and without wanting to fix another (and will be explored further in chapter 6). It can, of course, include the sharing of your knowledge to help others along the path when invited to do so and always giving from a place of abundance over scarcity, not holding back. It is important to remember, however, to check our intentions. We need to couple the giving with self-compassion and ensure that we don't forget ourselves! Giving to the point of exhaustion is a real sign of seeking external validation, to be "seen" as a generous person and people pleasing. A genuine and authentic intention is important for true generosity to exist. Otherwise, the giving is an act that is coming from a desire for something in return, even if it's just a feeling of approval, self-satisfaction or superiority. I believe everything we do is either based on (1) fear and scarcity or (2) love and abundance and although to the external world the resulting outcomes may look the same, the internal felt sense of the experience in the body and mind of the giver will be vastly different.

## Non-Judgement

I used to be so judgmental, of everything and everyone, not least of myself. And like most things, judgement is useful in moderation. It is a natural inclination for the mind to judge, as a mechanism to keep us safe and protected. When humans lived in the wild and faced the real danger of being killed and eaten, the mind needed to decide quickly if something entering its environment was a threat or not. However, in modern society, for obvious reasons, this instinct is much less useful, but unless we manage our mind, we continue to allow it to judge and assign almost everything we encounter with a quick, simplistic label of "good" or "bad", "right" or "wrong". This old way of protecting ourselves is unsuitable for our society now. In fact, it causes great divides amongst us, as we give other individuals and groups simplistic labels such as bad or wrong. Seeing them as threats, just like some angry tiger waiting to eat us. Judgement creates "sides" and an "us and them" in the world.

Yet we still allow the mind to engage in squarely boxing everything into neat categories because it gives us a sense of being in control. In mindfulness, we are invited to become more spacious and open, looking at different perspectives, not needing to take sides, or judge everything. Instead allowing things to be as they are, often just neutral. We are invited to accept and recognise the present moment as it is, without judgment, resistance, or the overlay of mental concepts. It takes energy to judge and often triggers intense physical responses in the body from emotions like anger or fear; fear of things that we judge to be bad or wrong.

We can judge ourselves harshly too, be it around our behaviours, bodies or feelings. We expect ourselves to be perfect, forgetting that by our human nature, we are imperfect beings. We can start an internal war with ourselves through our judgemental self-talk. Examples for me were, "you are so fat and ugly, how would anyone like you", "that was so embarrassing", "you're so stupid Eilís!". When my mind produced such thoughts, my body experienced them as enemies triggering intense emotions and pain in my body. Heartbreaking sensations in my chest or tightening in my stomach from shame. The mind and body at war. When our heart and gut want to be heard but the head is disconnected, misaligned, and making unhealthy judgments, internal suffering arises. Ironically, most people if asked would say they want peace in the world and yet can't even create it in themselves. Non-judgement is key to peace internally and in the world. It needs to start from the inside out; from the individual, to family, to community and then to the world level. But it starts with ourselves!

## Non-Striving

Striving is an aspect of modern life that, I have found, most people believe will create great success. I was a firm believer in striving myself for so many years. There seems to be an underlying belief that the harder we work, the more we get. Again, that certainly applies to a certain point but beyond which, we become unproductive and burn out. For me, striving implies not being aware of our limits, being unable to create healthy boundaries and being so out of touch with our bodies that we never know when to balance the stress with rest. There is often a subconscious notion that if we are not struggling towards our goals and through life, that it's just not going to be good enough or that we are lazy. I'm not quite sure where this belief comes from, but I suspect a mix of misunderstood religious teachings and a throwback to the mentality that kept the industrial revolution alive were part of it at least. It's an attitude that is often subtly supported and encouraged by large employers, who are trying to squeeze costs and increase profits by treating their employees like machines. There seems to be no appetite for an easeful, creative approach or any appreciation for quality outputs that might grow and flourish through flow and enjoyment of the process. No, instead working to deadlines through gritted teeth, furrowed brow, blood, sweat and tears is the method promoted to achieve acclaim. What a myth!

The most creative people ever existed took their time and periods of rest to attain their genius in their chosen fields. I can't imagine Michealangelo ever updating a traffic light scorecard at the end of each week with his progress on the Sistine Chapel. In fact, so many of the greats are known to have recognised the importance of rest and took breaks from their intense work to recharge and foster creativity. Whether it was long walks (and not the *Killnaskully Women* speed walking kind btw!), that Einstein, Darwin or Beethoven engaged in or short naps throughout the day, which Thomas Edison, Salvador Dalí and Winston Churchill all fostered to enhance and maintain their creativity, productivity, and overall well-being. Instead, modern-day workplaces are typically characterised by their fast pace, franticness, busyness, with back-to-back meetings, productivity targets, cost cutting measures and, of course, deadlines... there's always DEAD-lines. Sometimes I get the sense of the hamster frantically running, "busy" spinning the wheel but wonder what's really being achieved other than keeping each other busy by pushing work around in circles via email.

**Non-Attachment**

Another attribute that I have learned causes significant hardship is attachment; attaching to things, beliefs, identities and even people. In terms of materialistic attachment, it is completely understandable how habits like hoarding and excessively saving for a rainy day were strong traits in the generations, which experienced war, poverty and hunger. But this intergenerational trauma of scarcity, lack and the importance of holding onto everything for fear that there would be no more to follow is again, to a large extent, no longer relevant in today's western society. Fortunately, there is a lot more abundance when it comes to basic needs being covered for most of us. Yet we apply the same "holding onto" mentality to so many aspects in our lives.

We hold tightly to our beliefs, having to "stick" to our opinions even when new information becomes available because we have created an identity for ourselves around the belief. Phrases like "That's just not me", "I never" and "I always" are indications of this inflexible attached way of being. Similarly, attaching importance to material items such as the "big" house, "big" car, "big" job as symbols of our perceived status, identity and importance are forms of attachment. When any of these things are lost or damaged in any way, we can experience a lot of suffering. It's the same suffering from attachment that we experience when we resist the physical signs of the inevitable aging process. Everything is impermanent and when we inevitably have to let go of these attachments, there is resistance, and when there's resistance, there's suffering. We resist against the inevitable – the grey hair and the wrinkles – as opposed to allowing it to be as it is. There's no stopping it and ironically the stress of not wanting it will likely exacerbate the pain of the loss!

Impermanence and change are indisputable facts of life and they require us to be adaptable as opposed to having this more fixed mindset. When we become still we can see that life is often inviting us to let go of our resistance in order to create space for something better to come in, to grow and expand our lives. If we recognise the fact of impermanence of things and hold everything lightly, not grasping onto or clinging to them, then we allow more ease and flow into our lives. As Jon Kabat Zinn says, you can't stop the waves but you can learn how to surf!

>  **Situation + Resistance = Suffering**
>
> Situation + Resistance = Judgement in the Mind + Contraction in the Body

## Patience

Learning how to surf life's waves will, of course, require another foundational attitude of mindfulness, namely patience. In such a fast-paced world fuelled by technological advances, it is another trait in danger of extinction. There are ever growing expectations for instant results in all aspects of life and modern-day terms like fast food, instant messaging and Instagram are a testament to this type of living. The notion of delayed gratification is a dying concept and there is often a visceral restlessness in our bodies when we aren't getting instantaneous results. A mindful approach incorporates an understanding that sometimes things must unfold in their own time, that the flow of life cannot be hurried. We can see in the areas of health, diet and fitness that for long lasting, transformative lifestyle changes with no negative side effects, it is necessary to implement consistency over taking the quick fix crash diet or weight control pill. Mindfulness is no different in this respect. It requires discipline, consistency and a willingness to trust and wait for the benefits to unfold in their own time.

Eilis O'Grady

## Trust, Beginner's Mind, and Letting Go

I'm going to tell a story to illustrate some of the remaining foundations of mindfulness that guide my life nowadays. I think this story particularly shows how Trust, Beginner's Mind, and Letting Go play out in my new way of being… the new Eilís…

On the 5th April 2024, I left Broemountain, Co. Waterford for an adventure, flying to South of Spain and not having a return ticket – flying into the unknown, so to speak. I didn't know how long this adventure was going to be (still don't!), I didn't know anybody there, I didn't know the language and I'd never been to the area where I had booked an Air BnB for a one month stay. But from my mindfulness toolbox, I had trust and there was a knowing inside of me that this would be ok especially because the 5th April, although I wasn't aware of it when I booked the flights, was a special day. It was the 2nd anniversary of the passing of my good friend "Pat" (Patricia). She was a lovely lady whom I had had the pleasure of working with when I was in my accountancy role in one of the multinational companies. She was always a great friend to me and with her being 20 years older than me, often a source of wise counsel to me too. We were both enthusiastic about health and fitness and she would often be the one to nudge me towards the direction of the on-site gym if she noticed that my mood was dipping. We were unofficial accountability buddies in relation to our diets and we would rarely allow it to be said that either of us had succumbed to the temptation of the chips in the canteen. A healthy rivalry in every sense of the term.

At the time my friend passed away, I was also half way through the two-year part-time Masters in Mindfulness with

UCC. Pat had always been so excited and interested in the changes and improvements I was making in my life since my episode of burnout. She had seen me at this rock-bottom point and she witnessed the day that I had, uncharacteristically, picked up my handbag after a morning meeting and marched out of the office, reeling with anger to go to the doctor's surgery. Through my studies of life coaching, yoga and mindfulness since that time, Pat saw the significant changes that were happening in me. I will never forget the day she met my brother (in Café Bliss, Abbeyside) for the first time and after introductions were made, asked him, "So what do you think of the new Eilís?"

In her early sixties, herself and her husband were looking forward to stepping back a bit from their successful careers now that their children were adults and all very well set up in life. In late 2020, she and her husband secured the purchase of a beautiful spacious holiday apartment in Dungarvan looking out over the bay with amazing views of the sea and the Cunnigar. I really felt that this was going to be the entry of the good semi-retired life for her – the life of retirement that they had saved and worked hard for. Pat, unfortunately, never got to see her retirement, dying at the age of 62 years young on the 5th April 2022. On that very day, my own house sold in Abbeyside and I knew it was a sign that my life was going to take a very different direction… as long as I was open to it and as long as I did not allow the harsh learning that came from my dear friend's death to be lost on me. I had two choices really: (1) I could continue on the safe path, stay with my "good, pensionable job" as an accountant in a pharma company, which (despite what my annual performance review might suggest) was not my passion. It was a way to earn a pay cheque while working with some really lovely people but very little more, or (2) I could assume my retirement and pension were not guaranteed to me (which was made blatantly clear given Pat's death) and take that leap of faith into the unknown; following just a little heart whisper.

As a first step with this new perspective on living (and dying), I requested a career break to complete and ENJOY! (a radical concept at the time, I know!) my final year of the Master's program. The old Eilís would have pushed through, working long days and trying to squeeze in hours of study in any free time available in evenings and weekends and making the whole thing a big struggle. I was blessed with a lovely boss, who not only granted me the leave but supported me in all aspects of the handover…thank you Ciar. So the plan was laid out… I would take the college year and return in June 2023 to start a job share with my good friend, Emer, another great supporter and positive influence in my life. I enjoyed the space I had created for the studies as opposed to trying to squeeze and shoehorn study hours into an already hectic schedule, including work and running some evening yoga classes. Otherwise, I could have ended up at the door of burnout again! Now that would have been ironic given that I was studying <u>Stress Reduction</u>. I'm pretty sure such ironies are not unheard of though in our culture and society, which glorifies busyness. As I mentioned already, there seems to be a perception that if you are not tearing your hair out with stress, that you are lazy, selfish and/or somehow a failure in life.

Anyway, back to the story and like the saying goes, "if you want to give God a good laugh, tell him your plans" … a few months before my due return date to work, my friend announced that she was pregnant. With job share plans now scuppered, it made it slightly easier to take the decision to jump into the unknown, resign my position and explore mindfulness and yoga (which I prefer to call mindful movement) as a full-time career. I ran classes in community halls, schools, companies, residential care centres, indoors, and outdoors, for men, women and children. Taking imperfect action and trying out all opportunities that came my way.

Making leaps of faith as you can probably tell by now, was becoming a habit. So closing the loop from where I started here… having had a lovely winter of running classes, I leaped again and this time onto a plane to Malaga. Why Malaga? Well I googled destinations out of the nearest airport, Cork, and picked a place with the likelihood of some better weather. Not much thought is required really when you are open to an adventure. Another learning that mindfulness has helped me realise… body-based gut and heart decisions are more often than not more healthy than head-based alone… or at least characterised by a lot less effort, stress and overthinking. Having the capacity to trust your gut, like all good relationships, does assume that you are in regular contact with your body, listening to it and in-tune with its needs through daily practices such as yoga, meditation or journaling. Stillness is essential to hear what the heart is guiding you towards but such a rare state of being in modern society unless you can become intentional about creating it. Stillness is gold if you learn to mine it.

**Storytime..."Maybe"**

There was once an old farmer, who farmed his land with crops for many years. One day his horse ran away. On hearing the news, the neighbors dropped by. "So sorry to hear of your misfortune", they said sympathetically. The farmer replied, "maybe".

A few days later, the horse returned back to the farm and with him a few wild horses. On hearing the news, the neighbors dropped by. "What great fortune!", they exclaimed. The farmer replied, "maybe".

The following day, his son tried to ride one of the untamed horses, was thrown, and broke his leg. The neighbors again came to offer their sympathy on his bad luck. "Maybe," answered the farmer.

A few weeks later, soldiers from the national army marched through town, recruiting all boys for the army. They did not take the farmer's son, because he had a broken leg. The neighbours shouted, "Your boy is spared, what great luck!" To which the farmer replied, "Maybe".

This little parable shows how we have choice in how we interpret every situation. We can see events as "opportunities" or "disasters" and it shapes our emotions and the way we experience life. It also shows how we can never truly know how a situation will unfold. When we cultivate the ability to let things just be as they are, without having to judge as right/

wrong, good/bad, black/white, fortunate/misfortunate, there is a lot more space, more choice in how we respond. We can experience the freedom, ease and peace away from automatic reaction and judgment.

 **Pause, Breathe, Reflect**

- Are there any situations in your life where you could take a wider view and perceive in a different way to produce less suffering in your life?
- What foundations (non-judging, non-striving, letting go, allowing, trust, patience, gratitude, generosity, beginner's mind) of mindfulness might be useful in approaching these challenges?

# CHAPTER 3 – PRACTICING THE PAUSE

*"If you want to be happy, do not dwell in the past, do not worry about the future, focus on living fully in the present."* — Roy T. Bennett, The Light in the Heart

Being present means being able to live in the moment outside of the virtual reality of future and past thinking and mental chatter. The ability to be present is a super power and essential to enjoyment of life.

### Pleasure and Power of Being Present

In having the capacity to be present and approach (as opposed to avoid) life's more challenging moments, we can respond articulately and learn something from them. Suffering always offers an opportunity to grow if we can remain open enough to be with and process it fully. This means physically, we are able to allow the emotional pain to complete its natural cycle, i.e. pass through without getting stuck in the body and the ability prevents any long term negative health impacts. Resisting difficult emotion (energy in motion) leads to contraction and the negative energy being held in the body. The capacity to process emotions in a healthy way is cultivated through a regular practice of stillness, in which we step out of autopilot, pause, connect in and attend kindly to the inner experience. By sensing into the body and becoming aware of the felt sense of the moment, we are allowing ourselves to heal from the hurt. This is discussed in more depth in later chapters.

The ability to be fully present also enables us to wholeheartedly engage and enjoy the richness of even the seemingly smallest of things and appreciate more of life's pleasant moments. In being present, we are not letting the mind rule, taint or even ruin an otherwise pleasant experience by its constant compulsion to judge and box every moment into either right, wrong, good, bad. Instead, if we can be present, we can more accurately determine if this "feels right" for us right now. In addition, the mind might overlook the richness of a moment by either being in or referencing to the future or the past. For example, driving through beautiful countryside on the commute to work but not taking it in and enjoying it because the mind is already in the 9am meeting rehearsing what it's going to say! As I developed the skill of presence, I felt a renewed childlike awe for the world as I started to notice the simple pleasures in life that I had previously overlooked and missed in the pace of the day's human doing. Seeing nature transition through seasons that I didn't remember noticing much before or enjoying the sound of birds singing outside my window in the morning are just some of the joys that presence and a beginner's mind enhanced my life with.

With this increased proficiency for taking in the senses, there can be a heightened awareness of not only pleasures but pains also. Pains that may have been previously numbed with addictive behaviours such as comfort eating or over working to distract from the felt sense of reality. People can experience rude awakenings of how things really are and how they are showing up in the world that are causing suffering for their bodies, minds and maybe even those around them. They begin to see what a huge role their own mind plays in creating suffering, more suffering than is necessary, by judging, criticising, avoiding and resisting what is unfolding in their lives. There's a concept called the two arrows that comes from Buddhist teachings, which illustrate how we often amplify our suffering through our reactions to life's inevitable challenges. The "first arrow" represents the initial pain or difficulty—whether it be physical, emotional, or circumstantial—that is a natural part of the human experience. This pain is often unavoidable and outside of our control. However, what causes even more distress is the "second arrow" we inflict upon ourselves. This second arrow is our reactive, emotional response to the first—things like rumination, self-criticism, blaming, anger, or fear based over thinking. Instead of being present, approaching and processing the initial problem, we layer on this additional "optional suffering." This second arrow exacerbates our pain and can make a situation far worse than it needs to be. By recognizing this tendency, we can learn to face challenges with more equanimity, accepting the unavoidable first arrow without adding unnecessary suffering through our mental reactions to it.

I think a good illustration of this is my historical experiences of hangovers from a few too many drinks the night before. 1st arrow: There was the physical pain of the alcohol processing through my system, the headache or whatever other symptom there happened to be. 2nd arrow: But the whole experience was exacerbated and compounded by the critical voice in my head berating me for being "so stupid" or trying to convince me that I made a "right fool of myself last night", and "how will I show my face ever again". If energy hadn't been wasted on the 2nd arrow thoughts, maybe my body could have recovered the physical pain of the 1st arrow a lot quicker! In any case, the suffering was doubled by my thoughts.

> 💡 Pain + (Critical, Negative Thoughts) = Suffering
> (Pain +/- Suffering) + Kindness = Compassion

## De-blobbing Experience

Our life experience is an accumulation of moments. And, as mentioned earlier, in talking about what sitting meditation highlights to us, each moment of our lives is just made up of a combination of (1) sensations, (2) impulses, (3) thoughts, and (4) emotions (SITE). Yet these are the simple elements that we are judging and trying to get away from when we experience difficulty. When we break moments down in this way, we learn that there is nothing to be feared and we can approach and work with each of these aspects when they arise. In allowing the dust to settle in the present moment, there's more clarity and we can start the process of "de-blobbing" our experience. When the components of SITE arrive together and we don't have the capacity to isolate them into their individual component parts to see them for what they are, it is easy to become overwhelmed by what seems like a monster of physical, mental and emotional reactions grabbing hold of us. In mindfulness, we train ourselves to identify the parts of experience and name them separately. We see that what looks like a hideous monster, is in fact more of a gentle giant trying to help us out of a potential danger or threatening situation. There is nothing to be feared, only understood and when we have the tools to work with each element, it can become easy to diffuse a potentially overwhelming event.

> **Exercise – Take a pause, come into stillness, and maybe lower the gaze or close the eyes as you ask yourself:**
> - What **sensations** am I feeling in my body right now? Can I describe them?
> - Are there any **impulses**? Maybe to scratch an itch? Maybe to open my eyes if they are closed? Maybe to reach for my phone if it's beeped with a notification?
> - What **thoughts** are passing through my mind? Thoughts of doing this exercise?
> - If there are any **emotions**, can I feel where they are impacting my body?

If a situation arises and a flood of SITE elements arise, see if you can identify each of the parts:

1. SENSATIONS: Start with becoming curious around the sensations being noticed in the body. Where is the

sensation arising in the body? What is the texture of the sensation? Is it hard or soft or prickly or tingly etc.? What is the size of it? Does it have a color? A shape?
2. IMPULSES: Without acting on the impulse, can you notice the reactionary impulses to maybe push or move away from this situation? Just noticing that it's present without the need to do anything about it. Staying present as best you can. Like not scratching an itch…notice how it might dissolve in intensity when you can just pay attention to it fully.
3. THOUGHTS: What are the nature of the thoughts that are arising? Are they the second arrow type thoughts, adding to the initial pain and creating more suffering than might be necessary?
4. EMOTIONS: Go back to the body sensations. Where is this emotion being felt in the body? What is the sensation like? Instead of the more reactionary and impulsive habit of getting into the story and mental chatter around the emotion, such as how it was triggered or calling out blame or judgements about it, try as best you can to stay present with the body sensations associated with it.

**Practicing the Pause**

Taking the briefest of pauses in the present by anchoring your awareness in the body can transform an automatic fear-based reaction into a measured and authentic response to a difficult situation. It can be the difference between igniting a blazing fire of anger or cooling things down to quench a smouldering ember. I often use the analogy of receiving that nasty or threatening email, that I've no doubt we've all experienced at some point. And our immediate reaction is to pound out on the keyboard a strongly worded piece of our infuriated mind. However, one long deep exhale can be just enough to switch off the impulse to fight and instead find our ground before taking the next action from a place of steadiness. Having the courage to be with the unpleasant can be hugely powerful. Introducing informal moments of practice throughout our day to reinforce the habit of practicing a pause will increase the likelihood of being able to pause in the heat of an emotionally charged moment. Taking time to savour a deep breath between meetings, feeling the sensations of your feet as you walk to the water cooler, or soaking in the visual delights of nature from your window, are all accessible and effective ways within the many moments of a day to embellish the fabric of life and practice the pause. We can even become comfortable with and savour moments of silence and stillness – an almost radical act within the frantic society we live in nowadays.

**Introduce informal moments of practicing the pause throughout your day:**
- Take a few rounds of deep calming breath between meetings
- Notice how your body feels physically as you converse and interact with people throughout the day

- Feel the sensations of your feet as you walk to the water cooler
- Soak in the visual and audible delights of nature from your window.

## Creating Balance

In such as fast paced world, it may feel like going against the tide and it takes determination and strength in character to practice. We can get swept up in the speed of modern living, which seems to be accelerating rapidly with advances in technology. There are fewer natural opportunities for mindfulness and I am reminded of the comedian Des Bishop and his skit on mindfulness, where he talks about having to rewind the video cassette before returning it to the video shop and watching condensation drip on the window of the bus before the advent of smart phones. It impacts every area of life. I have gotten a grocery shop delivered to my door within 30 minutes of ordering, never mind a takeaway! Most organisations have year over year productivity metrics to reach (to ensure the share price keeps growing to fill the pockets of investors). This drives a work culture of having to get things done faster and faster. Unfortunately, after spending 8 hours+ a day working at a head spinning pace means that unless one is very intentional and aware, the driven doing mode spills over into home life and we end up doing everything in the same restless frenzied manner… inhaling food, power walking for 'relaxation', racing around the kitchen, getting kids organised to attend multiple activities to prepare for multiple games, attending social events to keep everyone happy, multitasking and ending up in a chronic state of stress. There's simply no balance unless we create it and this is where the practice of mindfulness comes in.

We talk a lot about wanting a balanced life or longing for a good work/life balance but not taking the responsibility to create it. We must realise that balance is not something that happens by itself, it's not something we can buy off the shelf, but rather something that we intentionally need to produce for ourselves. I frequently begin a class by welcoming participants into the space and encouraging them to take a few moments of appreciation for themselves for taking the time out to create balance in their lives. By showing up to practice they are creating stillness away from busyness, calm away from, sometimes, chaos and coming into the mode of human being away from, what can feel like the relentless, human doing of life. There is always something to do – one of the downsides with living in a world of such abundance and choices. When we come to our meditation chair or cushion, we are setting a specific time aside where there is nowhere else to be and nothing else to do. It is sometimes like the settling of a shaken snow globe, our minds and bodies are invited to slow down. Without the frantic doing energy stirring a storm of sensations, thoughts and emotions, there's a lot more clarity and we can see what we have been carrying around with us or what we've been trying to run away from. We might see that we have been exerting and exhausting ourselves, engaging in too many energy draining activities and realise that we will need to balance that exertion with some resourcing and energy giving practices (more in chapter 7 on this). In addition, we might come to understand that we have been disrespecting our physical, mental and emotional limits and it's time for re-setting and maintaining our boundaries.

 **Life balance check-in:**
- Bring stillness to balance busyness,
- Cultivate inner calm within external chaos
- Recover and rest after periods of stress
- Come into human being to balance human doing

Finding balance in all aspects of life is key to health and wellbeing and a skill to be practiced. How we do something is generally how we do everything. However, in a world of such abundance, it is often not easy to achieve moderation or balance and the tendency is to end up falling into extremes such as over-doing and over-consuming. There is always an infinite amount of food choices available to eat, there is always an infinite amount of work to be done, there is always more money to be made, more events to attend, more clothes to buy and more things to have. The term "moderation" has almost a negative connotation assigned to it and not something that sounds very attractive to most. As a consumer driven society, we are made to feel that more and more expensive is always better. Commercial advertisements instil a sense of lack and capitalise on the resulting vulnerabilities it creates. The most obvious sector to illustrate this point is the fashion and beauty industry, which are heavily dependent on women, in particular, feeling inadequate or needing improvement. Companies profit by exploiting insecurities, particularly those related to appearance, self-esteem, and societal expectations of beauty. The logic goes that if women universally woke up feeling confident and satisfied with themselves—without feeling the need to change, buy products, or adhere to certain beauty standards—a significant portion of the consumer demand that drives these markets would disappear.

We can see the extreme behaviours around our food consumption are producing serious physical health issues. The World Obesity Atlas 2024 found that in the UK, nearly 28% of adults were classified as obese by 2023, with projections indicating further increases. It warns that if current trends continue, the number of adults living with obesity worldwide will nearly double by 2035, with a significant portion of this increase occurring in Western countries. This has a direct correlation with cases of heart disease, stroke, diabetes and cancer. Over consumption is literally killing us as a society.

The same type of extreme approach is brought to making money and working. We exhaust ourselves to burnout in the pursuit of more money, which we believe will make us happier. Yet researchers have found a "happiness plateau" exists whereby while having enough money to meet basic needs and reduce financial stress is crucial for happiness, once a comfortable standard of living is achieved, other factors such as relationships, health, and a sense of purpose become more important in determining overall well-being. Ironically these are the life factors that are damaged most when extreme work practices are engaged in. So from a wider perspective, working to excess in an effort to earn excessive amounts of money is not only potentially fatal but also futile in the pursuit of happiness. It could be said that the imbalance turns the term "working for a living" into a contradiction.

## Human Being

Balancing the modes of being in the world, namely human being and human doing, is also essential for well-being. There is a time and place for both approaches to life – ideally an equal measure of both. The problem that modern day society finds itself in is that it seems to be submerged in human doing and has lost its knowledge of and capacity for the skills of human being. We live out our days on automatic pilot and disconnection, where our bodies are engaged in one activity and our minds in another. Our minds are typically lost in either the future or the past. I think of the old commute to work, 45mins of driving thinking about the day ahead, the meetings I was going to have and the task list I needed to get through. All the while my body was driving through the most amazingly colorful countryside. I would arrive in the carpark and not even remember the journey! Like "how did I get here!" Automatic pilot is wonderful in so many ways. If we had to re-learn how to tie our shoelaces every day, that would be hugely inconvenient and draining. But when autopilot mode is taken to the extreme, as with most things, it causes problems and we can end up blindly going through life with our head and body misaligned from each other. Lost in our heads or like James Joyce describes in A Portrait of the Artist as a Young Man, "Mr Duffy lived a short distance from his body".

When we are so detached from our body for long periods of time, we become de-sensitised to our reality. Our senses become distance acquaintances more than trusted friends. When we are living in our heads all of the time, we are rarely in the present moment and instead caught up in the unreal dimensions of the future or the past. It is simply impossible to experience a full life in this way. The elements of our full selves need to travel together in the same direction. However, what happens in unawareness is that the head is in the driving seat and life is passing us by unfulfilled; always with that feeling of lack and something missing… and there is… the heart and body. It's like the head has left them on the side of the road somewhere and continuing on the road trip adventure without them.

The head shy's away from difficulty and situations that stir emotions and that's understandable because it is not well equipped to deal with them. However, the body and heart come into their own in working with and processing such events but again, if they are not on-board and we don't have regular access to them, our minds decide to avoid, push away and supress unpleasant emotionally charged experiences. The mode of human being is about being in regular contact with the full of our bodies and invites us to approach all experiences with interest and openness. We come to know that we have the inner strength and resources to meet with whatever obstacles or apparent road blocks come our way so that we can progress and continue the road trip of living, learning and growing. This way of being embraces everything as either a moment to enjoy or an opportunity to learn, no experience is to be pushed away or denied and everything is allowed and welcomed.

Thoughts are the products of the mind, which as we have discussed is mainly consumed with the virtual reality of the future and the past. Yet if left unchecked, we can believe that our thoughts are real. Mindfulness proposes that we become more discerning about the credence we give to our mental outputs and invites us to take a look at our thoughts and build a healthier relationship to them. Human being mode is where we can see that thoughts are not facts, and so we don't get so caught up in them. I find it helps to see some thoughts as no more than waste outputs of another organ (the brain) of our bodies, just like urine from our bladder or sweat from our skin pores. We don't have to believe thoughts, identify with them, act on them or react to them if we choose not to. This is the nature of mind management and a crucial skill for whatever we want to experience in life.

When we become more detached from our thoughts and less identified to them, we can open up to take account of the wisdom arising from other areas of ourselves, namely the body senses, heart and gut. There's a whole field of other factors to consider outside of the often narrow focus of the thinking mind. When we take a wider perspective by opening up to the diverse contributions from our whole being, then we can see that we have more choice and options available to us. In addition, as it is a more holistic inclusive "all-party" type discussion with head and body, it is more likely that we will take an action that doesn't hurt any part of us. For example, if the head is left to it's own devices, it can take action to numb out it's aversion to difficulty like over eating and over drinking, which can damage the body. Whereas a more holistic all-encompassing approach to the ups and downs of life, will likely result in healthier choices being made and bring about more wellbeing and ease. We need to decide if we operate with the dictatorship of the mind or the democracy of the whole body to progress us forward.

## Continuous Manufacturing

When I began practicing mindfulness and noticing my thought patterns, I realised that I tended to be in future thoughts a lot more than thinking about the past. I wondered if this was in some way, my mind protecting me from re-living some of the pain of the past. And while this is likely to be part of it, I also think now that it is a lot to do with my work of over 20 years. The job of a financial accountant involved a lot of planning, forecasting and budgeting into the future. Each year, no matter what company I was employed at, the process for setting the company's budget for the following year was probably the largest project of the year and could start as early as July! It was a major effort to gather information from all the departments, understanding what was driving their spend requirements, rolling it up to company level, and only to realise that the combined total number was not meeting the target for the site set by headquarters, usually in the States. Then we would have to go back and start the process of cost cutting across the areas, while ensuring supporting cost saving measures could be put in place to achieve such cuts and, at the same time, ensure we rolled up to the prescribed budget target that would please the market and have a favourable impact on the share price. All of that to say, by December of a given year, I would already feel like I was half way through the following year; after 6 months of analysing and running scenarios for projects and cost improvement efforts that would be made in the following year.

Left unchecked, my mind remained in the future outside of work hours too. It's like it got stuck in a default of analysing the future, which was great for work but detrimental for personal life, not being able to savour the present and always looking to what was coming next. A sense of the present moment not being enough and it needed to be more, were likely other ways that my work contagioned into my personal way of being. I think it is important for everyone to be aware of how they need to show up at work and regularly ask whether this way of being is helpful for them in their personal relationships. Just as examples, if someone is in a role of authority at work for eight hours a day, does the person intentionally step out of that role before walking into their home to meet their partner in the evening? If not, could this way of being be negatively impacting on the relationship whereby there is a role of a leader being assumed and consequently their partner being seen as a subordinate? Or maybe someone is an engineer, for example, paid to fix issues and problems all day, every day and then carries that way of being into personal relationships, forgetting that they don't need to fix other people's problems outside of work all of the time.

Modern workplaces can be synonymous with stress and busyness, with deadlines, targets, metrics, and measuring productivity levels from all tasks (which will generally be expected to be improved upon the following year). Many will be familiar with the term "continuous production" or "continuous manufacturing", an approach characterized by the nonstop operation of manufacturing equipment, allowing for an unceasing flow of production materials and outputs. Bringing this mode of being into personal life, we can forget the joy of simply being in life and just participating in an activity for the sake of it, without any need to compete or produce anything. Unaware and unable to switch off the mode of doing, many will leave work on Friday evening only to engage in highly competitive sports at the weekends; more results driven activity. Even non-competitive activities like exercise and walking are often taken on with an attitude of striving; an intention to burn a certain number of calories or reach a target level of steps a day. Even kids after school activities are competition filled. I've heard of under-nine teams having more weekly training sessions than professional footballers leading up to "important matches". It seems like this results driven mindset is being instilled at a young age and on the other hand we are surprised at the ever increasing stress levels of the younger generation.

## Niksen

Again, I believe, all of this stems from an unchecked sense of fear and scarcity, which at a point in our history was very relevant as our ancestors struggled to attain basic needs such as food and shelter. Nowadays, our challenge is to let go of this out dated mindset and create a new one that is more fitting to the conditions of our current environment. Research has shown over recent years that the Dutch are one of the happiest populations on earth. One of the factors found to have contributed to this enviable label is their perfecting of a practice called "niksen", the art of doing nothing! An alien concept to many, I know! The word means 'to do nothing or deliberately do something without any purpose or goal of productivity'. This could be lounging around, listening to music, or looking out the window. Doing nothing, but with a purpose to do nothing or no purpose at all, may help to decrease anxiety, bring creativity to the surface, and boost productivity. It seems doing nothing is certainly better than being busy doing nothing.

In contrast, at an Irish funeral, it would not be unusual to hear statements such as the following given as compliments and in high praise of the deceased. "She/he was a great worker", "Sure she/he was great, they never stopped working", or "They worked themselves into the ground". High praise indeed! The underlying notion is that the more work they did, the greater their suffering and the better they were as a person. To me it now translates into the glorification of betraying one's own needs, being the martyr and people pleasing in search for external validation to feel valued in the world. Carry over behaviour from war times again? I'm not saying that it's not virtuous to help a neighbour but, like we spoke about in chapter 2 around generosity, only when it's given with a genuine intention, not expecting anything in return and when it's not at the cost of one's own wellbeing. Expecting praise or thanks and then not receiving it, will lead to the negative energy of resentment being the outcome. From directly living the experience of seeking approval from others through my work, I know that no matter how I appeared on the outside, the internal experience included striving, resistance, and often bitterness when I didn't get the level of adulation I had expected. Even when I did get the praise, it was a temporary buzz and I was soon on to hunting down the next opportunity for approval. This repeated cycle is exhausting and it is little wonder burnout results.

I sometimes wonder is it that we are trying to be Jesus-like in some way to guarantee our spots in heaven by crucifying ourselves and is it all some misunderstood religious rhetoric fuelling these types of actions. I think in my own case this may have been the intergenerational belief that was handed down and, not knowing any different, I translated into believing my value was measured by how much other people liked me. Although I was making myself sick in my diligent process of seeking approval from others, I couldn't see that there was anything wrong with it… there was an underlying belief that we were put on the earth to suffer and the more the better!...this was just the way of the world…I thought!

 **Storytime…The Business Man and The Fisherman**

The parable of the Mexican fisherman and the American businessman is a classic tale to demonstrate many themes including work life balance.

There was once a businessman who was sitting by the beach in a small Spanish village.

As he sat, he saw a Spanish fisherman rowing a small boat towards the shore having caught s good few big fish.

The businessman was impressed and asked the fisherman, "How long does it take you to catch so many fish?"

The fisherman replied, "Oh, just a short while."

"Then why don't you stay longer at sea and catch even more?" The businessman was astonished. "This is enough to feed my whole family," the fisherman said.

The businessman then asked, "So, what do you do for the rest of the day?"

The fisherman replied, "Well, I usually wake up early in the morning, go out to sea and catch a few fish, then go back and play with my kids. In the afternoon, I take a nap with my wife, and evening comes, I join my buddies in the village for a drink — we play guitar, sing and dance throughout the night."

The businessman offered a suggestion to the fisherman "I am a PhD in business management. I could help you to become a more successful person. From now on, you should spend more time at sea and try to catch as many fish as possible. When you have saved enough money, you could buy a bigger boat and catch even more fish. Soon you will be able to afford to buy more boats, set up your own company, your own production plant for canned food and distribution network. By then, you will have moved out of this village and to the city, where you can set up HQ to manage your other branches."

The fisherman continues, "And after that?"

The businessman laughs heartily, "After that, you can live like a king in your own house, and when the time is right, you can go public and float your shares in the Stock Exchange, and you will be rich." The fisherman asks, "And after that?"

The businessman says, "After that, you can finally retire, you can move to a house by the fishing village, wake up early in the morning, catch a few fish, then return home to play with kids, have a nice afternoon nap with your wife, and when evening comes, you can join your buddies for a drink, play the guitar, sing and dance throughout the night!"

The fisherman was puzzled, "Isn't that what I am doing now?"

The fisherman pointing out that he is already living that life now, without the stress and years of striving.

 **Pause, Breathe, Reflect**

- What are the skills, attitudes and strengths that are required for the work you engage in daily?
- Can you notice how this pattern of being may be showing up in your home/personal life? Is it helpful or unhelpful?
- Is there a need for more balance to be created?

# CHAPTER 4 – BEING IN THE BODY

*"In order to change, people need to become aware of their sensations and the way that their bodies interact with the world around them. Physical self-awareness is the first step in releasing the tyranny of the past."*

— Bessel A. van der Kolk, The Body Keeps the Score: Brain, Mind, and Body in the Healing of Trauma

By bringing awareness to how stress impacts the body and learning more about the science behind the stress response, we can begin to better understand how to manage it in our lives.

## Our Relationship With Our Bodies

A key part of the mode of human being is the capacity to sense into our bodies and inhabit our bodies more often as opposed to living in our heads all of the time. The more we are getting paid for using our minds, unfortunately, the more our modern workplaces lend themselves to "being in our heads". For example, industries like agriculture and farming, which historically required intense manual labour, are now characterised by large machinery from harvesting crops to milking cows. Quads and tractors take the place of having to walk in the fields and documentation and recording for quality assurance takes up a lot of the "saved" manual time. So increasingly as the population gets paid for using their minds, it's only logical that we are spending more time living in our heads. However, when we are not working, we are also tending not to be in our bodies, stuck on autopilot, we forget to return back to them. We are losing access to the immense power and wisdom available from the body by our dis-connection from them. It's like a long distance relationship more than an intimate one.

We are making things worse by being harsh and critical towards our bodies. We tend to want and expect them to be in a certain way while striving after perceived "perfectionism". Always quick to compare to some unrealistic, airbrushed and photo-shopped ideal, making for the basis of a very contentious and dysfunctional relationship. Recollecting what I used to say about my body when I was growing up (i.e up to and including my thirties!), my heart breaks. It was nothing short of verbal abuse! If I had spoken to anyone like I spoke to my own body, they would have had a good case for psychological torture. I dreaded the summer months because it wasn't as easy to cover up my body with clothes. Even living in Spain now, spending a day at the beach is still something I'm struggling to overcome and get comfortable with. I wore high heeled shoes as much as possible despite the discomfort, and often times pain, because I hated how short my legs were and I even ended up having to have surgery on my toe to counteract some of the damage done to my poor feet!. I plastered on make-up to hide behind (I know, I'm still working on this one!). And, even now, on the rare occasion that the scenario arises, I can still feel very awkward and nauseous approaching dancefloors from fear of being seen. My self-worth was measured in stones and pounds on the weighing scales and I was constantly punishing my body for never attaining the desired number (this still creeps in at times too!). I couldn't look at a beauty magazine without the running commentary of hateful comparison. It has taken a lot of work to re-build a more loving relationship with my body, the pain runs deep and I continue the work every day now to treat, nourish and relate to my body in a kind way. I would say this friendship still needs more work to fully repair and I know that by virtue of the tears in my eyes right now, releasing more pain as I write about it.

Mindfulness invites us to spend more time in the body, visit it regularly like you would a good friend. Getting to know and investing in the relationship between me and my body is key if I want to be able to "trust my gut" or "follow my heart" with greater confidence. When we build a good relationship like this, we can harness more health and wisdom. We can use the body as a barometer for incoming emotional disturbances and hear the whispers or sense the early warning signs of some unease physically or emotionally. We are thereby better placed to counteract issues so that they don't grow to be a bigger problem, when our bodies need to scream to be heard. Physical pain and emotions in the body are like inbuilt alarm bells alerting us to the fact that something needs attention, something needs to be taken care of and when it is looked after with gentleness and kindness, the pain tends to dissolve, soften and release.

I'm not sure was it a another way of being carried on from war times in Ireland but growing up following GAA teams (and even playing ladies football myself), it was clear that when a player played through injury it was applauded by most. Phrases from the side line and mentors alike of "good (wo)man, keep going, you'll be grand, no fear of you", "push through it, you're nearly there" are not uncommon. Half your leg could be falling off and it would make no difference. But where are the backroom team and supporters when you are having your hip prematurely replaced at 35! Workplaces aren't much different. The glorification of the striving beyond physical, mental and emotional limits is real in many organisations. Unfortunately it is highly unlikely that someone will come tap you on the shoulder and say, "you're exhausted love, go home for yourself, you are more important than any superficial deadline here". People who are strong on keeping healthy boundaries around their work time are more likely to be branded with the derogatory title of a "clock-watcher".

More trouble comes when we ourselves are not aware of what our body's limits are. When we have no connection, we don't realise what our bodies are saying and trying to communicate to us. If the body is being over extended in terms of its capacity, then it sends subtle signals at first, like little whispers. When we either are unaware of, ignore or cover over the body's messages over days, weeks, months and even years, it will inevitably lead to "dis-ease" and eventually disease. In order to hear the messages, we need to get quiet and connect in with the trusted friend of our bodies regularly through stillness or meditation practice. The body is such a powerful tool when we get to know it. Researchers are proving that the gut-heart-brain axis is an interconnected system where the gut microbiome, nervous system, and cardiovascular system interact to influence overall health, yet when we don't have the capacity to tune into the gut and heart, we cannot optimise our potential… essentially we are just firing on one cylinder out of three!

The body has a language and we can tell a lot about our own or someone's internal world if you can read it. Shoulders up close to ears are evidence that there's tension and resistance to something, sparkling smiling eyes suggest joy, fast paced walking might indicate a busy mind state, a tall broad posture may indicate confidence and a dry tight throat may point to the inability to express oneself fully. Being able to read body language is a key skill to develop if we want to improve our communication with others because as we will learn in chapter 6, up to 93% of interpersonal communication is thought to be non-verbal!

It is also useful as a tool for our own emotional regulation. We can leverage our own bodies to regulate our mood and mind states. Here are some examples to explore:

- Smile to feel happier
- Relaxing shoulders down away from ears to feel more relaxed
- Deep breath with long exhale to calm nervous system
- Loosen and open up hips, dance or shake to release stuck emotions
- Slow paced walking to quieten a busy mind
- Move to feel unstuck
- Producing sounds like humming or chanting to stimulate the vocal cords can have a calming effect on the nervous system.
- Standing tall, taking up space with wide base to feel confident
- Planting feet firmly on the ground to feel more connection and a sense of stability
- Self-hug or hand on heart to comfort and feel safe

> 💡 Tension can gather in your body throughout the day from thinking, concentrating and stressful situations. Taking regular pauses in your day to release this avoids negative consequences of build-up in the body that can lead to headaches or injury:
> - Softening your forehead
> - Unclenching your jaw
> - Relaxing your shoulders

## Fight, Flight, Freeze

In chapter 2 we discussed our innate instinct to judge experience as a historical way of protecting ourselves from dangers in the wild as hunter gatherers. Modern day tigers come in the form of angry emails, heated discussions with our colleagues, a poor performance review from our boss at work, getting stuck in traffic on our way to an important meeting or a child throwing a tantrum, etc. If we are not aware of it or don't have the capacity to mindfully manage these situations, they can trigger the same stress response in our bodies as a zebra running from a tiger in the jungle! Our nervous system switches on the same fight, flight, or freeze response as animals do when under a perceived threat. In preparation to act, the body muscles contract, the blood flow is re-routed to hands and feet for fighting or running, and adrenaline is released into the bloodstream giving a sensation of "butterflies" in the stomach. The hormonal surge increases heart rate and blood pressure, enhances alertness, and readies the body for quick action. As a result, non-essential functions such as digestion are temporarily suppressed, which can lead to physical symptoms like dry mouth and trembling. This acute stress response, while essential for survival in dangerous situations, can become problematic if activated too frequently or inappropriately in response to everyday stressors.

And even worse, we can get so used to operating on this mode (as opposed to "rest and digest" mode, where all body systems are functioning as usual) that we think it's "normal"! We are not aware that our bodies are in stress response and therefore take no measures to re-balance and take care of ourselves. Animals shake off and rest after a hunt if they are not killed, whereas unaware humans can remain in a chronic state of stress, moving from one deadline or chaotic situation to the next. Even the word "dead-line" brings to mind the image of a flat line on a heart rate monitor in a hospital and the alarm bells ringing to indicate that time has run out for the patient. This stark imagery suggests there is a perceived critical nature within the professional tasks at hand, where meeting it can be a matter of success or failure, life or death. When deadlines become a regular expectation of employees to work to, it is little wonder how they find themselves in a constant state of stress, leading to disease in the body, and possibly facing the medical "deadline" a lot sooner than necessary. Prolonged periods of chronic stress inevitably wreaks havoc with a person's health, numbing the senses and literally switching off vital systems in the body to conserve energy for the chase…the chase of the rat race.

> **Exercise – Where are your emotions felt in the body?**
> - What areas of your body get stirred up when stress/difficulty arises?
> - Where in the body do you feel anger?
> - Where in the body do you feel fear or anxiousness?

## Processing Emotions Through the Body

The mind is amazing and absolutely essential to plan, strategize and solve complex logical equations. The mind is great for work issues but when it comes to resolving personal emotional issues it is highly underqualified. Yet, frequently, we forget to switch off the automatic tendency when emotion arises and we jump into the mind for a fix, solution or a strategy to get rid of this threat or discomfort. Not only does this reaction not alleviate the emotion-based difficulty, it actually makes it worse and can trigger a vicious cycle of rumination and suffering. Mindfulness invites us to approach difficulty through the body, and not to be afraid of feeling the associated emotions it brings up in us. It invites us to get curious as to where this emotion is presenting in the body and when we locate it, to soothe and care for it like we would a small child.

**The following are the basic steps that I take:**

1. Name it (to tame it). If you can, name what the emotion is. What is it that's arising right now? What's this weather system – anger? fear? frustration?

2. Allow it (it's ok for this to be here). I acknowledge that it's ok to feel this emotion. This is all part of being human. I remind myself that there is nothing to be feared only to be understood. Maybe even offering kind phrases like "it's ok, this will pass".
3. Sense it (in the body). Where am I feeling this energy in my body? Anger is typically felt in the chest and fear in the stomach. Maybe the heart is beating faster, there's contraction in the muscles, heat in the chest, or nauseousness in the stomach. Does it have a shape; colour; size, big or small; edges, a start and an end; a texture, sharp or soft? Just bring curiosity to the felt sense of it in the body. You may notice that as you bring your attention to it, that it changes, moves or even dissolves.
4. Care for it (like a sick child). Particularly if the emotion is intense, maybe offering a gentle soothing touch, placing a soft hand on the area that is being impacted by the emotion. Can I create space around the area by way of maybe directing a breath into it, deep breaths with a longer exhale to bring the nervous system out of the stress response and back to calm. Or physically opening and stretching if I notice the body contracting. Remembering that emotion is energy in motion and by creating space for it, it will pass through the system more easily and complete its life cycle of arising, lingering and fading away.
5. Continue from a place of grounding and steadiness: Resting awareness on the anchor or the breath or body sensations, I can cultivate steadiness for myself and from

here, I can choose what to do next. From here I can ensure that my interactions in the aftermath are not marred or coloured with the negative energy that was stirred in me.

> 💡 Emotions are processed through being with the body. Going to the head for a solution only increases suffering. Thinking can be an avoidance strategy borne out of a fear of feeling emotion.

## "Turn off the Immersion!" - switching off the stress response

For those of us of a certain age, I often think, if we could channel the attention and diligence we gave in switching off the immersion switch in the 80's to our stress response, we would be doing a great service to our bodies. For anyone, who may be of generation where the call for "turn off the immersion" is not familiar, here's a brief summary…In the 1980s, immersion heaters were a common household appliance used to heat water. They were highly effective but also notoriously energy-hungry. To save on electricity bills, families were vigilant about switching off the immersion heater when not in use. It became a household mantra to "turn off the immersion," ensuring that the heater didn't run unnecessarily and waste energy.

Similarly, our stress response system, while effective and necessary for dealing with immediate threats, can become detrimental if left on for prolonged periods. Just as leaving the immersion heater on would waste energy and lead to high bills, constantly staying in a state of stress can deplete our energy and harm our health. By learning to manage and "switch off" our stress response when it's not needed, we can conserve our physical and mental resources. The most effective and accessible way to calm the nervous system is through taking in a deep breath through the nose and then a long slow exhale.

> 💡 It's helpful to take a few rounds of deep belly breath during the day to ensure that the nervous system has periods of rest away from stress:
> - Breathe in through the nose slowly, directing the breath deep into abdominal, belly area. Maybe imagining inflating a balloon in the belly.
> - Allow a slow, long exhale. Inviting the exhale to be longer than the inhale is key.
> - Exhale can be taken through the mouth to add an extra sense of release and letting go if needs be. Maybe even creating a sound of a deflating balloon through the teeth as you exhale.
> - Feeling the belly button deflate back towards the spine on the breath out.
> - A few rounds of this type of slow soothing breathing is ideal but even after one breath in this way, the body can feel less shaky.
> - Coming back to your normal rhythm of breath and notice how the body feels.

When someone involuntarily shakes or trembles after an intense traumatic experience, for example a car accident, this is part of the body's way of processing and releasing the stress and energy that was mobilized during the traumatic experience. It should not be stopped or interrupted as it is part of the natural healthy completion of the trauma cycle and helps bring the nervous system back into equilibrium. When undischarged energy remains in the body, it can lead to lingering symptoms of trauma, such as anxiety, hypervigilance, or PTSD.

Applying the same principle to less intense situations and daily stressors, the following are ways to recover and minimise after effects:

- Yoga – aspects of yoga such as breathwork and grounding poses can activate the parasympathetic nervous system (rest and digest mode) to feel calmer and stop the production of stress hormones. Stretching increases blood flow to tight areas, promoting healing and the release of toxins and stress-related by-products stored in the muscles. The hip area is noted for storing emotional stress, so hip opening poses can be especially effective.
- Earth and ground the feet – Our bodies are electrical systems, and the Earth carries a negative electrical charge. By coming into direct contact with the Earth's surface (e.g., walking barefoot on grass, soil, or sand), we can absorb electrons from the Earth, which may help neutralize free radicals and reduce inflammation. Some studies suggest that earthing can reduce levels of cortisol, the primary stress hormone, leading to a more balanced stress response and improved mood.

- Expressing difficult emotions like anger is healthy but expressing anger onto someone else is not, unless you have their permission. Yes, when anger arises, it's cathartic to scream, shout and/or let it out in some safe physical way but this can be done in private; no one needs to be around (and preferably not) for it to be expressed! (see chapter 6). Allowing yourself to cry is another way of releasing trapped emotions and there can be a huge sense of lightness and spaciousness in the body afterwards.

## Walking Meditation

Personally, alongside yoga, I find that walking meditation can be of great benefit in releasing high-energy emotions, such as grief, calming a frantic mind or in working with sticky thoughts. Monk and peace activist, Thich Nhat Hanh once said that walking meditation is like "kissing the ground with your feet." This beautiful image reminds us of the connection we can cultivate with the earth through mindful walking and the support the ground can provide us. The pace of walking can influence the pace of mental activity in the mind. When we walk slowly and deliberately, our thoughts tend to follow suit, creating a calmer mental state. Sticky thoughts, those persistent and often troubling ideas, can be particularly challenging. However, each time you notice these thoughts and gently anchor your attention back to your feet, the adhesive energy of the thought begins to diminish. The repeated redirection from the head all the way down to the feet gives a sense of de-centering from the thoughts and the ground serves to weaken the hold these thoughts have on your mind. Walking meditation can be very helpful to release grief, an intense emotion, which can be felt as an all-encompassing heavy energy throughout the entire body. Engaging in practices like yoga and walking meditation can promote emotional healing and well-being. The physical act of moving, combined with the mental discipline of mindfulness, creates a powerful synergy that aids in processing and alleviating the burden of grief and persistent thoughts.

De-centering or de-personalising from strong emotions is also very helpful. Unfortunately the English language does not easily lend itself to this and we often hear ourselves say, "I'm angry", "I'm sad" etc. The Irish language, however, offers a more helpful approach, which I like. Instead of "I am angry", it says "Tá fearg orm" (i.e. anger is on me) or instead of "I am sad", "Tá brón orm", which translates into sadness is on me. The former suggests a more permanent state or identity whereas the latter implies a more temporary status. Another view that is helpful is that of weather patterns, just like a storm of anger or a cold front of sadness washing over you and knowing that it will arise, linger and fade given time and space. When we identify with emotions and personalise them, we tend to go into a thought process that there is something more deeply wrong with us. Our heads start trying to fix and solve, which as we spoke about earlier, is futile. The emotionally charged jobs are best left to the body to process. So if possible relax and let the body complete the emotional clean-up operation.

## Afraid of Feeling

When I hear the phrase "I'm fine", I'm reminded of the *D'unbelievable's* comedy sketch on "Bridie's Christening". The sketch tells the tale of woe of a man after drinking two crates of Guinness and half bottle of whiskey. Each time his sister tries to intervene to advise him to take action out of the various predicaments he finds himself in, he replies stubbornly "I won't says I, I'm fine!". When I hear people reply with "I'm fine" on being asked how they are feeling, I sense the same blatant denial of reality might be going on. I translate the phrase "I'm fine" in this context as follows:

I'm ignoring my emotions and distracting myself because either (1) I don't know how to process or (2) I'm afraid to feel my emotions. Therefore I'm going to pretend they are not there and ignore them and get utterly distracted by either busyness, comfort eating, drinking alcohol, gambling, watching TV or whatever your distraction of choice is. I'm hiding away from actually feeling the emotion or tuning into what my heart and gut might be calling out for right now. Suppressed emotions get stuck in the body and will manifest in stress related illnesses down the line.

Addicted to busyness during the week and bars at the weekend is how I would have summarised my life at one point when I was in the thick haze of stress, burnout and depression. And it's no real wonder why I felt this was absolutely "normal" at the time – sure everyone was doing the same! Pubs were havens that allowed me to run away from how I was feeling and numb out. There had been no subject through school that had ever taught the skill of processing emotions in a healthy way. I found out about mindfulness in my late thirties and it was only then that I started to learn that our bodies contain the imprint of every single experience we have ever had throughout our lives. I learned that emotions are energy moving around in our bodies alerting us to something that needs to be taken care of and not ignored! That when we sit with emotions, make space for them, and tend to them that they can complete their cycle and pass through. It's when they arise in the body and their natural cycle is interrupted by defensive, disruptive behaviours that they cannot release out of the body and they get stuck but, as Bessel van der Kolk warns, "The Body Keeps a Score" or maybe more apt in the Irish context, the body will keep a tab for which someday a costly bill will be presented in terms of ill health.

 **Storytime... The Felt Sense Prayer**

Author Unknown – shared by Tara Brach
"I am the pain in your head, the knot in your stomach, the unspoken grief in your smile.

I am your high blood sugar, your elevated blood pressure, your fear of challenge, your lack of trust.

I am your hot flashes, your cold hands and feet, your agitation and your fatigue.

I am your shortness of breath, your fragile low back, the cramp in your neck, the despair in your sigh.

I am the pressure on your heart, the pain down your arm, your bloated abdomen, your constant hunger.

I am where you hurt, the fear that persists, your sadness of dreams unfulfilled.

I am your symptoms, the causes of your concern, the signs of imbalance, your condition of dis-ease.

You tend to disown me, suppress me, ignore me, inflate me, coddle me, condemn me.

I am not coming forth for myself as I am not separate from all that is you.

I come to garner your attention, to enjoin your embrace so I can reveal my secrets.

I have only your best interests at heart as I seek health and wholeness by simply announcing myself.

You usually want me to go away immediately, to disappear, to sleek back into obscurity.

You mostly are irritated or frightened and many times shocked by my arrival.

From this stance you medicate in order to eradicate me.

Ignoring me, not exploring me, is your preferred response.

More times than not I am only the most recent notes of a long symphony, the most evident branches of roots that have been challenged for seasons.

So I implore you, I am a messenger with good news, as disturbing as I can be at times.

I am wanting to guide you back to those tender places in yourself, the place where you can hold yourself with compassion and honesty.

If you look beyond my appearance you may find that I am a voice from your soul.

Calling to you from places deep within that seek your conscious alignment.

I may ask you to alter your diet, get more sleep, exercise regularly, breathe more consciously.

I might encourage you to see a vaster reality and worry less about the day to day fluctuations of life.

I may ask you to explore the bonds and the wounds of your relationships.

I may remind you to be more generous and expansive or to attend to protecting your heart from insult.

I might have you laugh more, spend more time in nature, eat when you are hungry and less when pained or bored, spend time every day, if only for a few minutes, being still.

Wherever I lead you, my hope is that you will realize that success will not be measured by my eradication, but by the shift in the internal landscape from which I emerge.

I am your friend, not your enemy. I have no desire to bring pain and suffering into your life.

I am simply tugging at your sleeve, too long immune to gentle nudges.

I desire for you to allow me to speak to you in a way that enlivens your higher instincts for self-care.

My charge is to energize you to listen to me with the sensitive ear and heart of a mother attending to her precious baby.

You are a being so vast, so complex, with amazing capacities for self-regulation and healing.

Let me be one of the harbingers that lead you to the mysterious core of your being where insight and wisdom are naturally available when called upon with a sincere heart."

**Pause, Breathe, Reflect**

- When you feel an emotion arising, can you notice where in the body it is being felt?
- Can you describe the sensation: texture, shape, size, temperature, colour, etc.?
- As you bring your gentle attention to it, do you notice that it might change, move or dissolve?

# CHAPTER 5 - KEEP KIND IN MIND

*"We hate suffering but seem to love it's causes"* - *Geshe Kelsang Gyatso, a Tibetan Buddhist monk and scholar.*

On exploring the habitual patterns of thought and behaviour that arise when faced with difficult times, we see how these modes of reaction can lead to more suffering and we look at how to reduce those stress inducing habits.

**Self-Talk**

After delivering several of the 8 week programs, it has been so rewarding and uplifting to see the changes that mindfulness brings to participants' lives and particularly at this point. Up to this point in their lives, some people never considered the notion of self-kindness before and I totally understand this from my own experience. The notion of being kind to yourself was somehow seen as selfish, in the Ireland that I grew up in at least. "Self-praise is no praise", or "She loves herself" were some of the biggest insults that could be levelled towards someone. The underlying societal message that, at least I took from this, was that loving yourself was a bad thing and from being a very rational thinker, I assumed then that hating myself was a more admirable personality trait. I remember one of the first things that the gift of self-awareness highlighted to me was my self-talk.

By the time I got to 6th class in national school, there were only 6 of us in the class, 3 boys and 3 girls. The two other girls were both naturally tall and slim and I was neither. In addition, my body was changing and I hated it. I had real resistance to everything around growing into adolescence, from having to wear a bra to the whole mess of periods, and to top it off, I was diagnosed and needed to be medically treated for severe acne! This was also when I first started to hear the comments around my weight and appearance. The remarks were coming from one person in particular, who I now see was only deflecting attention away from the pain of their own insecurities at the time.

The self-loathing and degrading comparison to others began in my head. I started, what I now call, the case book of evidence in my mind against myself to prove that the insults I was receiving were correct. I would say that this internal case book remained open until my very late 30's. I collected evidence in every situation imaginable to reinforce the idea that I was fat, ugly and unlovable. (Even writing this now even sends a sense of a dagger being stabbed into my heart, indicating that there is more work to do here). And for fear I didn't collect enough evidence, I began a mantra in my head: "I hate myself, I hate myself, I hate myself". For decades, this is what my inner dialogue was for any situation where I felt awkward or embarrassed in any way, which was a lot of the time. As a result, despite being good academically, I hated secondary school. I would crucify myself by comparing myself to all the "beautiful" girls, who were all dating and having the craic with the boys. I would literally make myself cry from hurting myself with insults (far worse than those ever given by the initial instigator) and reminding myself how fat and ugly I was. With mindfulness I realised that, unnoticed to myself for years, I had actually been practicing affirmations, but they were the highly destructive kind. Absolutely incredible when I say this now but that was a fact. Decades of emotional self-abuse!

Being a young girl, who really tried to do her best at everything, I took on this way of being to become very diligent at hating myself. I'm not sure how I was perceived from the outside. I suppose it depended on how close people got. My teachers rated me as diligent, hard-working and a pleasure to teach so there was definitely a good external cover to some extent being formed. That's the thing with being diligent, I was also very diligent in compiling my case book of self-hate in parallel to the school books, I became very good at proving that I was unlovable and also very good at covering it all up to the outside world. Internally I believed that only beautiful skinny women were destined for happiness in life. All the TV programmes and films fed right into my story too, it was a relatively easy case to build against myself. I would run to the bathrooms in Davitt's nite club while the slow set was on to hide my shame from having no boy to dance with. I bought all the diet books imaginable to try to lose weight but again I see now that this was futile given my running commentary of disgust with myself; it was only another thing that I could beat myself up for…another failed diet! My parents would encourage me to go for walks, but I didn't want to be "seen" on the road walking, too embarrassed about my body image. They must have been at their wits end. I remember Dad even agreeing to take me to "Weight Watchers" to see if that would help me. Of course, it was never the diet that was the problem, it was the internal dialogue that was holding me back from change. I held a strong identity to being fat and ugly and that's what emerged. Like the saying goes, whether you think you can or you can't, you are probably right.

Looking back now, it was like having an abuser residing in my head. Always reminding me of how I was falling short and comparing unfavourably to others. I could give hours crying in front of the mirror before going out, berating myself for being so fat and ugly before my poor mother would find me and console me back into a calmer state. Often I cried so much that I just couldn't go out. And even when I did, I spent many a time in the ladies toilets "hegging" from self-loathing while my friends were out dancing and enjoying themselves. I struggled with having, and later staying in romantic relationships, but how could I possibly love another when I hated myself so much – hindsight is a great thing of course. Obviously, through my recent work, I see that it is impossible to truly share with another what you haven't got for yourself. I really believe that the relationship with yourself sets the tone for all other relationships in your life. Having a good quality relationship with yourself enables good quality relationships with others and the world! I see now that I was incapable of real authentic friendship and love because I had absolutely none for myself and I forced great people out of my life through self-sabotage and not feeling good enough to be loved and treated well. The deeply ingrained belief that I was unattractive and unlovable was so strongly programmed in (by myself), that it ensured that I also unconsciously self-sabotaged diets and weight loss attempts too. It was a vicious self-maintaining circle of self-abuse through self-talk. Thoughts were creating my reality. If there was only one change I could recommend to someone within all the changes I have made since I was introduced to mindfulness, it would be to become alert to self-talk. If the voice in your head is not sounding like a supportive and trusted friend and/or a cheerleading coach, then change it…fast! Look in the mirror, congratulate yourself, support yourself and love yourself.

> 💡 A powerful exercise in working with harsh self-critical talk that has worked wonders for me was getting a photo of myself as an innocent child and sticking it on my mirror. Anytime I noticed the berating chatter begin, I ask myself "would you talk to this girl like this?" The golden essence of that little girl is still in me somewhere, so why would I?!

The internal inner critic voice, although harsh, critical and judgmental, actually originates from a desire to keep us safe from harm and failure. The inner critic serves a protective function. The only way to really become aware of the inner voice is to get quiet. It's hard to hear the inner critic in the noise and busyness of daily life.

## Exercise – Transform Inner Critic to Inner Coach

The following is an exercise to investigate the limiting beliefs of our inner critic and change them:

1. What is the Inner Critic voice saying?

*Example: You are not good enough to do this.*

2. Identify with your limiting belief.

To do this, personalise what the Inner Critic is saying – turn it into an "I" / "I AM" statement

*Example: I am not good enough to do this*

3. Get curious around what it is trying to protect you from.

Note: it is likely that this belief helped/protected you in the past in some way but ask whether this still serves you or if it is now holding you back?

*Example: Fear of failure and being judged by others was the fear underlying the inaction. However, this fear is no longer relevant to me because the people who matter don't mind and those who mind don't matter to me.*

4. Flip the limiting belief into a positive statement.

*Example: I am good enough. I can do this.*

5. Then note how that feels.

*Example: This feels empowering. I feel a strength and glow from my chest when I say this. I notice my shoulders broaden and my head lifts....*

> 6. Note how life would be different if you believed this new statement to be true and use the present tense to express it, as if it is already in place:
>
> *Example: I am healthy and fullfilled. My life is full of fun, laughter and happiness.......*
>
> Finally, it might be a good idea to use this new positive statement as an affirmation, repeating it regularly to reprogram the brain and firmly securing it into your belief system. Remember to use the present tense!

**Bring Compassion to Suffering**

Dad was a rock in my life. I admired him and loved him so much. I was so proud of him because he was kind, strong and was always helping people. He was held in high regard by everyone. On the 14th December 1996, I had come home from college in Limerick, where I had just started a degree in Business Studies and German in the University of Limerick (U.L.). Although the transition out of home for the first time was tough with not knowing anyone out of my school year going there, I was finding my feet by being blessed to share accommodation with a lovely farmer's daughter from Ennis, Co.Clare. We had so much in common and we were taking the same college course so we became great friends. I looked forward to the scheduled landline call with home from my digs or getting a call card to ring from the phone box during the week. That Friday night in December, after returning home for the weekend, I remember sitting in the living room in Broe watching telly while Dad sat across from me shining his shoes with "Mr Sheen" in preparation for going dancing later that night in Hanrahan's pub. He told me how he was so proud that I was in college. The daughter of a man who had went only as far as 4th class in primary school before he had to leave to go work on the farm at home and later onto the meat factory in Clonmel. He was thrilled that Elaine and Wally (Walter) were getting "top marks" in their school tests and were well set up for the Leaving and Junior Cert respectively. He was really chuffed, as education was his absolute priority for us. I guess given his own background, he may have felt he was held back somewhat by not having a better schooling. Later that night, while my Mam and Elaine were at a Christmas pantomime in Ardmore, Dad arrived home uncharacteristically early from Hanrahan's pub, where he and Mam would frequently go dancing. Our cousin brought him home because he said he wasn't feeling great. I said it was probably a bad bottle (of beer) and I'd mix up some "Andrews" to flush it out of his system. When I got to the bedroom he was on all fours on the bed in pain. All I remember is that he started to slip off the bed and he appeared to be suffocating, and as I tried to cradle him in my arms, I remember screaming for Wally. After that is a blur. I remember ringing our neighbors, Tom and Bridget Kiely, and I think they may have rung the ambulance or maybe I did…I'm not sure. Dad died of a massive heart attack on the bedroom floor that night surrounded by the paramedics.

 Absolute devastation ensued. It was an enormous shock to everyone. Dad was a fit, healthy man that gave so much of his time walking the hill to tend to the sheep and when he wasn't doing that he was either building concrete walls and home extensions for people or shearing sheep. People told me after that when they heard the news that they were sure that the name was wrong and that it had to have been Pat O'Grady, his older cousin across the road, that was after passing away. It had been Pat's plan to have Dad inherit the farm when he would pass but in the end, Dad died before him.

And for myself, I had another massive addition to my case book of self-hatred… the guilt of having my father die in my hands and not being able to save him that night. Again much of the following days, weeks, months and even years are a blurry haze. So much loss, so much grief, so much more hatred for myself. Added to the over-eating now, there was over-drinking and over-working as ways to self-medicate and avoid my reality. I increased levels and sophistication of self-sabotage in terms of my health and relationships. In parallel, I developed more refined layers of protection around myself and thereby, to anyone looking in, I seemed like a normal well-functioning adult contributing to society. I went onto studying in Germany as part of my college course, worked in an Irish Pub while I was there too, returning to successfully complete my honours degree and was offered a job as a Trainee Accountant in a practice in Limerick city. I'm sure for the most part, people encountered a smiling, friendly, pleasant individual. I had "good pensionable" jobs, nice cars, nice houses and even a long-term relationship at one point… with a saint of a human being I might add. I went about life following the rules and in accordance with expectations, achieving my professional exams and work-related goals along the way. Internally I was riddled with internal unease and pain, which I medicated and temporarily soothed with destructive and addictive behaviours.

Healing all of this happened (and continues to happen) through a combination of mindfulness and compassion. The overarching intention of mindfulness is to alleviate suffering. When we connect with ourselves regularly and get to know our bodies, minds and ways of being better, we can become more aware of how we suffer in life and how much of this suffering can be reduced because it is self-created! After learning and building the skill of paying attention and awareness of habitual self-destructive habits, we are then invited to explore how approaching difficulty in life with a kind and caring attitude might impact our experience. Bringing this type of approach is called compassion and is a hugely important concept in mindfulness when suffering and pain exist. Compassion is a word that comes from Latin origins, meaning "to suffer with". Compassion exists wherever kindness and love are applied to a situation involving pain and suffering at any level. This was a radical notion for me when I came across it. In the past, I dealt with pain by resisting it, not wanting it to be there, trying to push it away, distracting myself from it by blaming others or berating myself for whatever I was experiencing. I numbed out the pain with comfort eating, drinking or busying myself with work to try and forget it all. I didn't approach my feelings with compassion, I avoided them. I had no awareness of what I was actually doing, never mind ways to work with what was really present.

Nowadays, when I notice feelings like fear or sadness, I sense into where it is showing up in my body (usually stomach or heart areas) and maybe place a gentle hand there to soothe the tension or pain. I remind myself that I don't need to start analysing and reasoning out why this pain is here or who's to blame etc. I just need to sit and tend to the sensation of it for a while. Just like gently holding a child when they are crying. This creates a sense of spaciousness and there is room to just be with the sensations of the pain that have been stirred up and allow the energy to flow through its natural cycle of arising and fading. I imagine talking to a little girl living inside of me, saying things like "I've got you", "I'm here now, everything is going to be ok", "no need to be afraid". I see this as releasing similar painful energy that got stuck in my body when the younger version of me didn't have the tools to process these feelings. It's like parenting the inner child to let go of a piece of stored pain from the past that was re-triggered by the present event.

The origins of both mindfulness and (self-)compassion share a common intention to alleviate suffering. When we offer ourselves the same gentle caring attention and support that we might give a small child or a good friend in the same situation, suffering can soften and even dissolve. Recognising that all humans suffer, that we are not alone, and that pain is an inherent part of being human, and on some level, unavoidable. Knowing this releases the underlying unrealistic expectations of thoughts such as "I shouldn't be feeling like this" or "why is this happening to me" that so often arise in painful situations. It provides more space for reminding myself that "it's ok", "it's a normal part of every human life to feel pain" and "this too will pass". With this more accepting dialogue, away from the fighting commentary of the reactionary mind, our bodies and minds tend to relax, soften and open to allowing things to be just as they are for now.

> 💡 Some self-compassionate actions that we can take when faced with difficult or strong emotions might include:
> - Asking questions like, "how can I bring kindness to this situation?"
> - Offering self-soothing by way of a gentle touch, hand on the heart or to wherever the physical pain of the emotion is being felt.
> - Speaking in a friendly and supportive way with a soft and caring tone. "How would I speak to a good friend or small child going through this pain?"
> - Exploring "what do I need right now to take care of myself?"
> - Reminding myself of the impermanence of all experience and "this too shall pass."

## Loving Kindness Meditation Practice

"Metta" or loving-kindness meditation has been proven to be a powerful transformative practice in cultivating a more compassionate mindset and reducing stress. There are variations but generally involves repeating short simple phrases of well wishes such as "May you be happy," "May you be healthy," and "May you live your life with ease." This practice begins with directing these intentions toward oneself first, similar to the notion of attending to your own oxygen mask first before being able to assist others. There is a recognition that you cannot truly love another without loving yourself first, nor be kind to others without being kind to yourself. This practice can feel alien, awkward and, frankly, weird at first. Once a foundation of self-kindness is established, the practice can be extended to others: first to someone for whom it is easy to express kindness, then to a neutral person, followed by someone with whom you may have difficulties, and finally to all beings collectively. In the practice, we acknowledge that no matter how we or others appear on the outside, that we can all feel fearful, sad or lonely on the inside. In deliberately cultivating kindness by taking the time to wish ourselves well, we create a space for inner peace and compassion to arise that naturally extends to others. This process helps counteract the tendency to be harsh and critical towards ourselves and others, fostering a more empathetic and understanding perspective.

As you engage in this practice, becoming aware of your physical and emotional state is essential. Notice how these phrases resonate within you and how they influence your breathing. Each phrase can be a soothing mantra that aligns with your breath, enhancing the meditative experience. This mindfulness practice not only grounds you in the present moment through placing attention on the phrases being offered but also invites a profound sense of kindness and befriending toward yourself and others. The act of repeating these phrases—paired with awareness of breath and a focus on kindness—encourages a gentler and more forgiving approach to life in general too. It allows for a recognition of the humanity in everyone, promoting a deeper connection and understanding. By systematically extending well-wishes from oneself to all beings, the practice nurtures a boundless compassion that can transform your interactions and relationships, including with yourself. Squeeze an orange and juice comes out. The same for us; what's inside comes out. Concentrate (excuse the pun!) on filling up on light on the inside, and it will shine out naturally.

## Reactions to Road Blocks

When we're faced with stress or difficulty, we have a wide range of typical reactions in terms of thoughts and behaviours. Below are some of the associated words that have come up in sessions but it's by no means an exhaustive list.

Blaming, Angry, Scared, Alone, Lost, Stress, Prickly, Paranoid, Restless, Depressed, Ignoring, Trapped, Numb, Brooding, Withdraw, Sick, Anticipation, Guilty, Frozen, Agitated, Seething, Driven, Gittery, Detach, Pain, Tearful, Worthless, Rejected, Overwhelmed, Anxious, Frightened etc.

**There are many common avoidance behaviours such as:**

- Emotional eating and drinking
- Busyness
- Scrolling on the phone
- Binge watching TV
- Avoiding friends
- Working excessive hours to get on top of workload
- Constantly seeking approval and validation from others
- Gossiping
- Procrastination
- Thinking!!!

Through these unhealthy reactionary behaviours, we can easily find ourselves going round in never ending circles of suffering, like not being able to get off a roundabout. Like we discussed in chapter 3, where we looked at how we often add the "second arrow" thoughts to the initial pain or problem we face, serving only to create a bigger problem and more suffering. In a similar way, we can do this in our reactionary behaviours and actions too. We engage in unhealthy activities in an effort to patch over or avoid approaching a difficulty, which itself creates more difficulties. Everyone will have their own scenarios of how they get themselves caught in self-maintaining loops but here were some of my classic examples:

- Work: When I found myself overloaded at work, I would drop my healthy nourishing activities like exercise to work longer hours. Energy levels would go down as a result, I'd start eating more sugary food, drinking more coffee and I would begin to feel sick, tired and exhausted. From that, I was making mistakes more easily, which led to more re-work… more work! Oh, and not to mention the blaming, frustration, anger and bitterness depleting my already low energy on top of all that!
- Relationships: In experiencing dynamics that I didn't like in relationships, instead of approaching the situation in a mindful way (see chapter 6), I would keep my concerns stored up internally, worrying and ruminating. I was afraid to be vulnerable and feared conflict and rejection if I let my true feelings be known. As a consequence, the constant stream of ruminating would interrupt my sleep, leading to

tiredness and irritability. Ironically, these mood states would trigger major arguments about minor matters and with the core issue never being resolved, the relationship was bound for ultimate failure.
- Health: Another classic of mine was when I felt sad and lonely, I would comfort eat and binge drink, which would cause my body to feel unwell, heavy and lethargic. Consequently I would start berating myself, leading to more sadness and more disconnection from myself and others.

## Consuming Social Media, News and TV

Research has shown that there is a strong correlation between a harsh inner critic and the tendency of idolising others, whether it be on the basis of their seemingly flawless bodies, perfect lives, or number of followers etc. So it is little wonder that the constant exposure to curated images of success, beauty, and happiness on social media, movies and TV can exacerbate the self-critical self-talk habit. We perceive ourselves as falling short of these media-driven ideals and find ourselves engaged in striving after the illusion of perfection, which of course is a complete waste of precious energy. Perfection is an illusion, a phrase worth repeating! Perfection is an illusion! If we haven't cultivated a sense of our own self-worth from inside out (see chapter 7) and are constantly seeking external validation, we will continue to be a victim to the self-abusive behaviour of our social comparisons. We can take on false and damaging beliefs to exacerbate our victimhood, such as by measuring our self-worth by number of "likes", "followers" or so-called "friends". Believing our chosen idol is some sort of super human capable of avoiding pain or suffering, while forgetting that every single human on the planet is guaranteed to encounter pain in their lives.

What we are actually seeing on screens are avatars, which by definition are a digital representation of people existing in virtual realities. Each time we engage and get sucked into the cybernetic world, we join the avatars in that virtual reality. Mindfulness helps us build the capacity for regular reality checks and brings us back to the real world of the present moment, which like all of us humans, is perfectly imperfect. Through our practice we strengthen the capacity to take a more balanced interpretation of situations. We leverage the skill of noticing where our mind's thoughts have been carried off to and we can bring our attention back to what's real; the facts. From this point we can become curious around how we are perceiving this picture, reel, video etc., just as we learned in chapter 2. And remembering that perception is not reality. We start to ask what meanings, beliefs and assumptions am I applying to viewing this image that's resulting in my feeling inadequate and berating myself accordingly. A mindful way of engaging with social media like this might include ensuring to bring an attitude of gentleness and kindness to ourselves while consuming content. Also to take care of ourselves, maybe by balancing screen time with some real time, be that in nature or fully present with real physical human beings.

As much as I monitor what I eat for my physical health, I am mindful of what I consume mentally also. We all accept that having a pint and whiskey for breakfast everyday would badly damage our bodies. In the same way, filling up on negative news every morning is as damaging to our minds. Why would it be any different?! The phrase "you are what you eat" can apply just as much in this regard, i.e you become what you consume on a regular basis. And if the radio is blazing out negative news reports or the latest bickering row from the government chambers, you can be sure that negativity is entering your system at a cellular level along with your Weetabix. Being intentional and mindful about what you input into your physical, mental and emotional systems is important for maintaining balance, peace and ease. Daily news intake, the regular consumption of soaps or the latest Netflix series can be highly impactful due to their repetitive nature. The messages and "norms" of these productions are reinforced day after day or night after night and as such programming our minds into adopting them as part of our own belief system. Our minds don't easily distinguish the difference between fact and fiction and we can absorb and normalise behaviours that are being portrayed on these media unconsciously. We can also absorb the energy they emit. Have you ever noticed how your face is contracted and tight or that you are in bad form after an episode of Eastenders? And let's face it, it's not great for exhibiting compassionate communications either (see chapter 6). Having young adults (or any adult for that matter) adopt expectations of their sexual and romantic relationships from "Love Island" is unlikely to be a solid basis for healthy relationships. In addition, potentially devastating on their being able to form positive self-images for themselves. These are just examples of how consumption of regular media output can impact us, if it is not approached mindfully.

## Our words matter

Awareness of what we are inputting into our internal physical, mental and emotional systems is crucial in the pursuit of health, happiness and contentment. Your mind, heart and body will respond to nourishing or negative inputs accordingly. In terms of inner dialogue, as we know, the majority of our thoughts are repetitive and therefore how we speak to ourselves each day matters because the language we use will literally programme the software of the brain. I have a list of alarm bell words and phrases that when I catch myself saying anything from this list, I pause and reflect on what I've just said. Sometimes it can be appropriate for the context and absolutely ok but more often than not, the language can be unhealthy, untrue or even damaging to my health and wellbeing.

**Terms include:**

- "I always" / "I never" / "that's just not me": can suggest a fixed mindset, unwillingness to change or unwillingness to believe in the concept of neuroplasticity, and often used as a lazy way out of something we do not want to do.
- "I should": can highlight expectations and it's important to ask, who's expectations are these?
- "I should": can point to perfectionism, an illusionary concept that is so damaging, I've listed it separately.
- "I must": can highlight struggling for, resistance, going beyond physical limits, striving, forcing against.
- "I miss": (aside from grief, obviously!) can suggest living too much in the past and/or glorifying the past.

- "I thought": assumption based on a past experience, maybe indicating a frozen-in-time opinion of someone or something that might be well out of date!
- "They say you should…": can suggest blindly taking on the advice of "experts" or broad-stoke societal advice without consideration for one's own unique circumstances, body and life. Maybe question who "they" are, look up the research paper behind the advice and make an informed decision for yourself.

 Bring attention to when you say the word "should" throughout your day and ask yourself "who's expectations are these?"

## A Mindful Approach to Media Driven Ideals

"They say you should…". If you were to take all the "expert advice" about how to attain a healthy and happy life, then you would likely have no time to sleep in a day and "they say you should" get 8 hours! Taking the area of health alone, "they say that you should" eat x, y and z, and not only that but you should eat the "right" combination of macro- and micro- nutrients, at specific times of the day and measured in relation to your current weight. "They say you should" get x amount of exercise, and that you need to include weights, cardio, flexibility workouts and ensure that your heart rate stays within a specific range. "They say you should" not drink coffee, while others say coffee has numerous health benefits for heart and brain. "They say you should" get plenty of sun for vitamin D but avoid the sun to prevent skin cancer. etc. etc. etc. And these examples only cover the "they say you should"'s from one, of typically eight, segments on the wheel of life! Extend the same "expert" (and often contradictory) opinions to leisure, love, friends, personal growth, finance, career and home life and you have a real head melt of expectations for yourself!! And we wonder why we are stressed!!

To take a mindful approach, I go back to the basics when faced with challenges like this. The foundations of mindfulness (see chapter 2) are generosity, gratitude, patience, trust, non-judging, non-striving, curiosity, acceptance, and letting go. And here's how I might apply them to this scenario.

So first off to say, so much of this information is solid and as a society we are so fortunate to have it at our finger tips. I am so **grateful** to be living in an age and society where I am not struggling for basic needs... and I am also grateful for those researchers who have applied their passion and time to discover how we can make our lives even healthier and happier. Unlike our grandparents, or parents even, we live in abundance rather than scarcity and the struggle we face is really how to manage abundance in all aspects of our lives... from information overload to food choices.

I think acknowledging and **accepting** that we can't take it all in is the first step – no one can! There is a constant flow of new information being published and is quite simply impossible to incorporate the infinite stream of new knowledge. I am also **letting go** of the habit of taking on other's expectations and the broad-stroke societal advice. Instead more intentionally creating my own customised manageable set of standards for my health and wellbeing to the best of my knowledge, which is based on an equal balance of some "expert" opinion and, more importantly, on my own expert opinion of my unique body, relationships and life! I remind myself that I am the expert of my body and life and the more I take time to connect in with my body (e.g. yoga) and mind (e.g. meditation), the better my research analysis is, so to speak. Knowing that my body and life are changing all of the time means what might work best now might be different in the future, so being open minded and curious to what is being called for day to day, in the moment.

Also remembering that these "experts" are human, and as such imperfect and prone to inaccuracy and flaws like the rest of us. A minority of these "experts" may even be open to receiving the odd brown envelope from a big corporation to advocate for their product or service! So I **trust** my gut more, what feels right and that I know best for my unique self!

Last but not least, checking in regularly to my **intention**. If ticking the boxes to achieve countless personal health and lifestyle metrics is resulting in me feeling exhausted, unhealthy and unhappy, then it's defeating the whole purpose …that of cultivating health and happiness. Sometimes I can get so caught up in the box ticking buzz (an old habit from the corporate world) that I forget the "why" of the whole exercise. Regularly stepping out, **taking a wider view** and connecting with my intention keeps me on track more effectively than any traffic light scorecard ever did!

**Storytime... Dragons and Princesses**

We have no reason to harbour any mistrust against our world, for it is not against us.

If it has terrors, they are our terrors; if it has abysses, these abysses belong to us; if there are dangers, we must try to love them.

And if only we could arrange our lives in accordance with that principle which counsels us that we must always trust in the difficult, then what now appears to us to be the most alien will become our most intimate and trusted experience.

How could we forget those ancient myths that stand at the beginning of all peoples, the myths about dragons that at the last moment are transformed into princesses; perhaps all the dragons in our lives are only princesses waiting for us to act, just once, with beauty and courage. Perhaps everything that frightens us is in its deepest essence something helpless that wants our love.

So you must not be frightened, if a sadness rises up before you larger than any you have ever seen; if an anxiety, like light and cloud-shadows, move over your hands and over all you do.

You must realise that something is happening with you, that life has not forgotten you, that it holds you in its hands; it will not let you fall.

Why do you want to shut out of your life any unease, any pain, any melancholy, since you really do not know what these conditions are working upon inside you?

Rainer Maria Rilke

**Pause, Breathe, Reflect**

- Bringing to awareness a scenario where you may typically feel stressed. When you feel stress arising, can you notice what your habitual patterns of reactionary behaviour are? Blaming others, comfort eating, distracting with busyness, withdrawing from the world, numbing, ruminating, etc.
- How might you be creating more and/or maintaining suffering in this way?
- What might be a healthier approach to this stress?

# CHAPTER 6 – COMPASSION AND COMPANIONS

*"Be who you are and say what you feel, because those who mind don't matter, and those who matter don't mind."* — Bernard M. Baruch

Communicating with others and relating to the world around us with mindfulness and compassion can transform our experience of living.

**In Communication with Others**

Communication is a process of creating understanding and connection. In talking about generosity earlier, I mentioned the concept of mindful listening, which I summarise into three elements:

1. Intention – setting the intention of listening to hear and understand as opposed to the more common habit of listening to reply. There is often an automatic and unintentional urge to perhaps only focus on getting one's own viewpoint across. Reminding yourself that holding a safe space for a person to be fully heard without interruption or judgement can be the greatest gift of all to another.

2. Attention – giving full attention to the person, making eye contact and noticing body language and tone as well as words. While verbal communication is crucial, research suggests that when conveying feelings or attitudes, words may account for only 7% of the message, with vocal tone contributing 38% and body language 55%. Obviously the importance of verbal content is much higher for more factual discussions. In addition, being aware of the internal chatter of the mind and not giving it undue attention over the person speaking.
3. Attitude – checking in with the attitude and energy that is being brought to a conversation and being aware of how contagious these can be between parties in a conversation.

Often while we may appear to be listening to another, we are in fact, cognitively conjuring up our response. We often feel the need to try to fix or come up with a solution to what the other person is saying. Maybe noticing phrases like "I think you should…" or "what I would do is…" or "have you tried…?" We feel the need to relay our own experience of what's being said, often denoted by "oh that happened to me too when…". Instead, mindful listening invites us to stay present, engaged, attentive and resist the urge to interrupt. Even embracing moments of silence to convey that we are giving the other the space to express themselves fully. Other aspects of listening in this way might include summarizing back to the speaker what they said to confirm understanding and show that you are listening. Holding a physical posture that demonstrates attentiveness like leaning slightly forward, openness and avoiding crossing arms, which can come across as closed and defensive.

When I need to have difficult conversations with others, whether I'm inadvertently brought into one or preparing for a communication that I know will be uncomfortable, I keep in mind another key principle, namely grounding. Just like before taking a flight it's important to know how to attend to your own oxygen mask first before trying to help others. As best I can, I connect to my anchor of the breath, feet, or both to calm and steady myself so that I am best placed to respond in a mindful way; from a place of authenticity and real presence as opposed to becoming reactionary. A deep breath with a longer exhale than inhale can be just enough to settle the nervous system if it has been triggered into a stress response. Feet rooted onto the ground can offer that sense of composure and stability that may be required. Having the nervous system remain in the calmer rest mode allows for clearer thoughts, more creativity in response and generally serves as a superpower in tense situations.

From this point, I am better able to gather my awareness onto my intention, attention and attitude in the conversation. I hold the intention to listen to understand instead of listening to reply. And I remain curious about what the other person needs or wants, which could be external validation, understanding, or attention etc. Remembering most people just want to be seen and heard! Practicing a pause can be powerful and being comfortable with moments of silence can be hugely effective in terms of easing the tension of a situation. When there is more presence, there is more choice and less reactivity and with a continued steady presence and a non-threatening demeanour, it's possible to invite the potential "aggressor" into my calm as opposed to joining them in their storm of anger or fear. There is also more space to take a wider perspective, and question the interpretations, meanings, assumptions or judgements that I may be bringing which may be fuelling any hostility arising.

Practicing to take a deep breath and smile before answering the phone is another great way to pause and remind myself to remain open and present for whatever is coming my way in the call. There is absolutely no doubt that the skills involved in the art of real communication takes practice. As a coach I practice this all of the time and yet can still fall into the same old habits and roles at times, especially if there is intense emotions or tiredness present. Ram Dass, the spiritual teacher, once said: "If you think you are enlightened, go and spend a week with your family." That's where you can really test out your strength in this area. But, overall, as I improve and my skill gets stronger, I find it so rewarding in terms of less heated interactions arising and more enriching conversations being had.

In navigating arguments and difficult conversations:
- As best you can, can you invite the other into your calm as opposed to joining them in their storm of anger or fear?
- Use your anchor of breath/body/sounds to steady, calm and regulate your nervous system if you notice it being triggered. The anchor is also useful when you notice

> internal mind chatter distracting you from listening to the other person.
> - Express your needs using "I" messages, speaking about your feelings and thoughts and avoiding declarations about what the other person is thinking or feeling. These are non-aggressive, non-blaming, non-threatening and thereby avoid triggering others into a defensive stress response.
>
> *For example:*
> *Instead of "you are inconsiderate", try "I am feeling ignored"*
> *Instead of "you're a disappointment, try "I'm feeling disappointed*
> *Instead of "you're late", try "I feel disrespected"*
> *Instead of "you're making me angry", use "I am feeling anger" (own your emotions!)*

As stated in chapter 5, expressing difficult emotions like anger is healthy but expressing anger onto someone else is not, unless you have their permission. Yes, screaming, shouting, and letting it all out can be hugely cathartic, provided it's not directed to another. Hold these release sessions in private if you choose, no one needs to be around (and preferably is not) for it to be effectively expressed. It's your energy in motion, own it, release it and move on without expectations or needing anything from another. Sometimes we hold onto anger in the expectation of an apology or some other response from another person. If it comes, great, but either way let it go as holding on to the resentment energy only hurts you in the long run. The other person may not even know that you are angry. They may not even know you exist! Holding onto anger (or resentment) is like drinking poison and expecting the other person to die. Remembering again that emotions are energy in motion, if they are not released, they will reside (in the body) and they become very disruptive long term tenants! Storing excessive energy builds pressure which creates stress and can cause explosive breaks, just like storing gas in a tank.

## Healthy relationships

I have found that being intentional around surrounding myself with people who inspire me to be better, who contagion positivity and who energise me can enhance the quality of my life and health significantly. Just like food or news consumption, energy can be consumed quite easily by virtue of being in contact (in-person or virtually, as energy transcends any physical boundaries in this regard). When I over-do it on the "Haribo" jellies, I can feel an uncomfortable pulsing of sugar through my body similar to what I get when I've been in contact with too much negativity. In recent years, I had to start letting go to align with the person that I am discovering beneath the defence layers of protection that I spoke about in chapter 2. Sometimes this happens through natural drifting away by virtue of no longer being connected by a common interest (e.g. drinking) and sometimes it involves more intentional action to create more distance where a relationship is no longer nourishing. Like every aspect of life, impermanence applies to relationships too. Some walking companions will walk with you for a short time, others all your life and others again can come in and out at different stages along the road. Relationships are in the nature of changing and allowing them to ebb and flow through life stages makes for more peace and ease. When we attach tightly to them and try to force them to be fixed, we are doomed to failure. By their human nature, they are ever changing and so it's only natural that they may be "right" for just a while or at various times. The transition period after letting go is generally not easy. When I needed to let go of my drinking habit, it felt like a loss, a type of grieving process followed for the part of me and the people I was leaving behind and it was very isolating at times. Again with the help of mindfulness, I trusted that I was creating space for something new and healthier to emerge (such as a new tribe). It can be a slow process requiring patience (a key foundation of mindfulness explored in chapter 2) but so worth it in the longer run.

**Gossip**

Releasing old habits can have an equally freeing effect on physical and mental wellbeing. Becoming aware of daily conversations that I am involved in is another aspect of daily consumption that I give more consideration to. For example, do I listen to the same whinging, gossiping and moaning from the same individuals on calls, social occasions or at the water cooler every day? How does my mind and body feel as a result? Is it drained and depleted? Is this beneficial for my ongoing health or not? Could I choose better for myself in furtherance to my goals around health and stress reduction? There is always a choice. And gossip is a dirty habit that is unhealthy for all involved because of the toxic energy it produces. From reflecting on my engagement with it in the past, I realise that it is a distraction away from the tougher conversation that needed to be had at the time – the one with myself! But not liking myself and being afraid to look inside meant I was always kicking the can down the road. It can be very painful to discover the truths of how you are showing up in the world so it's much easier to engage in pointing out other people's flaws; bubble gum for the brain to keep us busy and away from the real work of introspection. It's like "look over there, look what Mary did…?" or "can you believe that Johnny said that?" to take the spotlight away from what you might see if you were the one being analysed so closely. It helps to remind myself that when my index finger is pointing out the shortcomings in someone else, that there are three fingers pointing back at me!

It's also very easy to get swept back into this old habit of gossiping and when I find myself in an environment where I know it's likely to arise, I need to be particularly attentive to my responses in conversation. It's a sneaky habit and, even now, it's often not easy to remain neutral in a society that seems to need you to take a side. Like a recovering alcoholic in a pub, the environment is going to make abstaining more difficult than usual, so in the same way, I try to avoid situations and people where I am likely to be enticed back into these unhealthy interactions. We can automatically slot into old relationship roles without awareness. Sometimes it's necessary to let go of these types of relationships if there's not a common intention to remove these bad habits in order to create a healthier dynamic.

Eilis O'Grady

## Making Connections

We often make friends in school and college and then, in general, we strive to hold onto these into our adult lives, even though the initial reasons for the connection are gone. We don't question why we still "make the effort" to meet up or whether the relationship is still healthy for us. As adults we might fear it will be too difficult to make new friends after years of having held onto old friends; another sign of our scarcity mentality perhaps! Our scarcity mentality can trick us into thinking that there will be no more if we lose relationships of any kind! But when we choose to live from love and abundance, we know there will always be more to come. From my own experience of moving to a different country in my mid-forties, alone and without knowing anyone when I arrived, I have found that I really enjoy making new friends who match my energy, values, and personality, who "vibe" with me as they say. Fear of letting go, fear of being alone, a lack of self-worth or confidence are other barriers of protection that stop us from allowing relationships to dissolve naturally. The older I get, the more I see how relationships can be such great containers for mutual nourishing, learning and growth when both parties have a good connection. In my view, making mutually nurturing connections or even creating sparks romantically, as the name suggests, happens when two people meet that are equally de-layered in terms of their personal development process, like two exposed wires without their insulated coatings that create a spark, releasing the light and energy and a current begins to flow between the two. I wonder is that why "young love" seems so potent; when the insulted coverings of psychological self-protection are so thin at that point and people are connecting at a level that is closer to their true essence, closer to the golden light at the centre of us all.

As a new, albeit smaller, circle of companions continues to evolve around me these days, I often remind myself that I can continue to love people but not like their behaviour and therefore I need to stay a safe distance away as I try get to know my own more exposed, real self. Their behaviour is just a layer of protection around them that they have created to keep their real selves safe. I have plenty of layers that still need to be brought to the surface of my awareness and begin the slow process of peeling them away to come closer to the most real and authentic me. All anyone needs to do is look at a baby or small child to know that we didn't arrive into the world with so much heavy protection around us and that our true essence is not as fearful as what the majority of people end up carrying around on their surface. I think most religions point towards more of a love and light at the centre of our being. Even for the atheist, there is no question that humans have fields of electric energy. We "connect" with others, we feel each other's "energy", we "glow", "radiate" when we feel good, "recharge" when we feel depleted and we "earth" and "ground" ourselves when the current of energy is strong and overwhelming, we can be "wired" and "sparks can fly" between people. The more I enter into de-layering, the more I seem to hear people say how "it suits you!" and I seem to be radiating better energy than the past. It's like there's more light getting through from inside with the masks and shields coming off. It's amazing to see how like energy attracts and connects and I am meeting more people who are similarly exposed in terms of the peeling off process and partaking in the work of discovering their inner selves. It takes time and everyone is on their own timeline. I know that while there may be a distance between me and some old friends now, I am confident that we will converge again along the road of life ahead and enjoy each other's company again with the new found wisdom we find in between. For now, betraying my own health and well-being for any longer than is necessary, by playing out the same old roles within unhealthy relationships, is just not an option. The cost is too high. If I want to fly and flourish in life, then holding onto anything that doesn't serve me any longer is like weighing myself down with stones hanging from my ankles even if there is a vague promise of a big financial lump sum pension at the end of it. The process of letting go, while not easy, will result in a life of physical, mental and emotional lightness, increased energy and flow.

**Producing Positive Energy**

Mindfulness has opened up my eyes to seeing that life isn't about accumulating things, people or even knowledge. It can be more about letting go and harvesting inner wisdom. Neither is it about suffering and pushing through hardships. Yes, it's true, pain arises in life and this is the only guarantee to a child coming into the world. However, our job is not to produce more of it than naturally arises. Our challenge is to dissolve the inevitable pain we encounter by meeting it with grace, gentleness and kindness. We bring an intention to learn from it without generating additional suffering and negative energy for ourselves or anyone else around us, who is likely to absorb our energy.

> 💡 I find it helpful to stay on track in any situation by asking myself two questions:
> - what is this situation teaching me?, and
> - in working with this, is my energy polluting the world around me or am I emitting positive energy into the atmosphere for beings to breathe in?

Finding this win-win scenario means there is no self-betrayal, no physical boundaries disrespected, while having positive intent for myself and others. That's not to say that others may not like the action I am taking but that's their challenge to process what learning they can take in their positive and authentic way. I can only take care of my energy and set my genuine intentions to grow and evolve without meaning harm to anyone. Others get fearful when we don't stay in our traditional roles, which we have acted out for many years. This fear can translate into anger towards us when we begin to choose more wisely for ourselves towards growth and sustainable health and happiness. So being brave enough to say "no" and peel off the people pleasing plaster is not easy but again, worth it in the long term to experience the benefits of healing fully.

Producing more positive energy requires a growth mindset, which is one of two ways of approaching life:
1. a growth mindset, sees life as a dynamic adventure, with the invitation to learn each day how best to sail with the waves of ups and downs in life and being excited for what's to come next, or

2. a fixed mindset, stuck in stubborn ways, fighting against the waves and resisting change and suffering the inevitable consequences.

The fixed mindset approach is one born out of fear. It will look like rinse and repeat, copy and paste or autopilot type living and is characterised by an unwillingness to see that change is inevitable. Like when you see an emergency situation on TV or in films, you will often hear something like, "everyone just stay where you are, don't move and it will all be ok". That works great in a dangerous situation as does the fight, flight, freeze response, which we looked at in chapter 4, but these are short term survival mechanisms and neither are designed for thriving and flourishing in life. It is very understandable for people living in war zones or in devastating circumstances to live like this of course but we, in modern Western countries, in the main, have no reason to go through our lives with this mentality. In relative terms, we have won the lotto with most of us enjoying modern comforts like hot showers, running water and a machine for every household chore imaginable. We sometimes forget that little over a century ago, most of the wealthiest royalty in the world did not have access to such conveniences and luxuries that we now take for granted. We are living in the future and yet applying survival behaviours adopted by our ancestors for dealing with the hardships and hazards in the past.

Given that impermanence is a fact of life, there is really just one option if your intention is to live with peace and joy. Approaching life with a growth mindset is almost like playing a computer game, we are given a challenge and when we have mastered the skills of that level, we can move onto the next. We progress by navigating the challenges that we encounter along the journey of life, picking up on clues, resourcing ourselves when need be and fearlessly experimenting and exploring the various options available. Being curious is very much part of the mindfulness ethos. Seeing things with a beginner's mind and fresh eyes every day, every moment and being open, willing and sometimes fearless to try new ways of approaching life events is definitely a healthier approach. And it's more likely to result in peace, ease and contentment for body and mind than using a fixed mindset. Asking questions of ourselves is a key skill on the journey of, not only self-discovery but living in general. It's important to have a healthy curiosity around everything we engage in and even more importantly to be open to hearing the answers and adapting accordingly. Everything is constantly changing, including ourselves, and we are continuously being met with new unique life circumstances that invite us to approach with a new unique combination of life skills. This is how we grow and learn; looking at each and every unique moment fully and determining what is the best action to move forward. Questioning why we are doing things, and not blindly following the crowd or doing things because "that's how they have always been done" is imperative to leading a fulfilled and happy life.

## Starting a Peace Pandemic

What goes in, comes out in some way, so by being more particular about what energy we fill ourselves with, will also ensure the likelihood of emitting similar energy into the world around us.

As mentioned, setting the intention to produce positive energy in everything we do creates a win-win for everyone involved. By meeting everything we encounter with an attitude of gentleness and kindness is a key learning in mindfulness and is in furtherance to this intention. When fear and anger is met with more fear and anger it just gets bigger but when they are met with compassion and openness, they lose their power. You will have to indulge me on this next bit but I often think, if we could somehow make this practice widespread, and if each of us started approaching our pain and meeting it with kindness, then positive energy would be injected into the world on a massive scale. As energy is contagious, we could start a pandemic of positivity and peace. Energy is not limited by borders or distance, like COVID 19 was, so imagine the rate that it could spread if distance wasn't an obstacle for it! If the energy of a single mobile phone can be detected in space, can you imagine the far reaching impact of the energy from one human being. By cultivating kindness and love in ourselves first and then just by being more of our true selves, our energy would radiate out spreading to near and far. Like we alluded to earlier, it would have to start internally, having our head, heart and gut aligned so that there is no internal disturbance and out of that soil, positive energy would naturally blossom. This would then spread into our close relationships, into our families, into communities and eventually further beyond. Creating peace in ourselves and easing our own internal battles will at least build a certain skill set that could eventually be scaled to a global level.

Hearing news from across the globe of war and ferocious atrocities has undoubtedly been difficult for all of us. I don't consume much of the news broadcasts on TV or radio but there is enough discussion and coverage on social media of world events to understand and know that there is a lot of devastation, pain and suffering ... there always has been. Feelings arising for me when I am exposed to the latest outbreak of war include helplessness, anger, fear, disgust and utter broken-heartedness, which I'm sure are common to most. There is an immediate impulse to want to take action (i.e. a reaction) but I remind myself that reactions arising out of variations of fear based feelings will only breed more fear, anger and resentment type energies. Fear feeds on fear. The fire of anger is fuelled by more anger and the flames can spread like wildfire. It would be so easy to take on the keyboard warrior mentality, solicit blame and criticise the perceived inaction of our elected representatives or whoever we are choosing to point the finger at but that's polluting the world with more negativity. Looking at social media, it seems some feel that the only way to change things is to get angry, not being aware of the poisonous energy they are emitting in the process. It's like fighting fire with fire in the name of peace! Knowing how powerful our energy can be and how fast it can transmit, if we could become more intentional about our actions and responses to prevent worsening the situation by adding fuel to the fire. We could consider ways to be proactive for worthy causes that are not, in fact, adding any more hate energy into the world's pot of energy. We are a clever species, could we try to pause and reflect on what these solutions might look like before the negative energy engulfs the good stuff?!

💡 Research has found random acts of kindness not only benefit the receiver, but the giver and even any witnesses to the act as well! Happy hormones such as oxytocin are produced in the body and one good deed in a crowded area can create a domino effect and improve the day of dozens of people!

Some ideas for Random Acts of Kindness:
- See how many different people you can smile at today
- Contact, send a message (or even a letter!) to someone to see how they are
- Look for something positive to say to everyone you speak to today
- Wish people you meet a nice day
- Turn off digital devices and really listen to people
- Buy extra at the shop and give to someone who is homeless
- Slow down to be kind, give people your time and full attention

##  Storytime... The World as Our Reflection

A traveler, weary from his journey, arrived at the gates of a town and met a wise woman sitting there. He asked her, "What kind of people live in this town?"

The woman responded, "What were the people like in the place you came from?"

The traveler replied, "They were a miserable lot—selfish, deceitful, and constantly complaining."

The wise woman nodded and said, "You will find the same here."

Later, another traveler approached the woman at the town's gate. He, too, asked, "What kind of people live in this town?"

The woman again replied, "What were the people like in the place you came from?"

This traveler said, "They were wonderful—kind, generous, and always willing to lend a hand."

The woman smiled and said, "You will find the same here."

What we find in others is often a reflection of what we bring with us.

**Pause, Breathe, Reflect**

- What expectations might I be bringing to relationships that could be putting a strain on interactions and triggering the other into a stress response?
- If I know I have all I need to be happy within me, why am I still wanting and needing outside of me?
- Are there unhealthy relationships in my life that I may need to distance myself from for a while to support my health, growth, wellbeing etc.?

# CHAPTER 7 – It's all up to you!

*"Your life begins to change the day you take responsibility for it."* — Steve Maraboli, *Unapologetically You: Reflections on Life and the Human Experience*

Taking responsibility for our lives by learning, implementing and continually practicing nourishing activities will enable us to live full, balanced and happy lives.

## Taking Responsibility

We exercise, get sufficient sleep and eat healthy if we want to maintain physical health and now we are going to take a look at how we can do the same for our mental health in terms of managing stress and mood. We explore how to create balance in our lives through the activities we engage in, balancing depleting activities with more nourishing activities. As we mentioned earlier, if we want a more balanced life, we create it and it is something that is well within our power to do. Like everything else it begins with awareness and then it's about taking the responsibility and positive, and often fearless, action necessary.

We look at how we can resource ourselves if the barometer of the body is indicating that there may be a low mood on the horizon. We can take preventative measures to ensure that a passing light shower of bad form doesn't turn into a prolonged storm of damaging depression. And again we are highlighted to the fact that so much is within our control. To a larger extent than we probably imagine, we can choose or at least positively influence how we feel. In the past, I would have pointed the finger and blamed others; my over demanding boss, the crazy driver on the road, the rude shop assistant, the untrustworthy government etc. etc. Nowadays, there is little that makes me wince more than when I hear someone say "They made me so angry" or "They hurt me". It's just so disempowering. I find remembering the equation, which we talked about in chapter 2, very helpful in relation to understanding what I mean here:

*Facts +* **My** *Interpretations = My Emotions + My Reactions = My Unique Reality*

This shows we control how we choose to interpret an event in our minds and as a result our emotions and subsequent reactions. Therefore, the power and responsibility lies with ourselves if we don't want to continue to feel a certain way. Yes, someone can trigger the arising of an emotion within us but after 90 seconds (the lifespan of an emotion) it comes within our control. Past 90 seconds, we are making ourselves angry, we are hurting ourselves by adding reinforcing thoughts to the initial triggering event.

> 💡 We can choose to stop giving our power over to others and external uncontrollable situations. We can start changing how we perceive and process triggering events to take our power back. It is useful to ask questions like:
> - What meaning am I giving to this?
> - Can I take a wider view and see it from another perspective?
> - Is a similar past experience clouding my judgement of this interaction?
> - What part am I (*or my thinking, more specifically*) playing in this that could be making things worse?

Yes, a classic case of "simple but not easy" but like anything, it is a skill that can be practiced and mastered to enjoy more agency over our lives. It enables us to choose how we want to feel.

A very simple everyday example to show how much choice we have over life situations might be how we relate to the weather. If our over-arching intention in life is to be happy and reduce unnecessary suffering in our lives, then why would we create a judgement thought in our mind that is likely to create a negative feeling in us. Yes, these are only small moments, but repeat it several times a day, every day and it adds up to a lot of moments with a downbeat pessimistic feeling in our bodies and minds.

<u>My overall intention:</u> to be happy and reduce unnecessary suffering in my life

<u>Fact / Uncontollable Event:</u> It is raining outside

<u>My interpretation/thought choices:</u>
- Positive options: Rain, essential for life and growth, nature, food supplies
- Negative options: Rain, I hate the rain, it's awful, I wish it would stop

<u>Resulting Reactions and Emotions:</u>
- Positive: Smile, feeling of gratitude, lightness in the body and happiness
- Negative: Furrowed brow, contraction and heaviness in the body. Mood dips, low energy.

(Either way, it's still raining outside!)

## Mountain Meditation

In-keeping with the theme of weather, there's a mindfulness practice called the Mountain Meditation. It is a practice where you visualize yourself as a majestic, grounded mountain, unwavering and stable despite changing weather conditions around you. Invited to sit tall, this guided practice encourages participants to embody the qualities of a mountain—strength, stillness, and resilience. This visual of a mountain experiencing all the various seasons and often harsh weather events and yet remaining it's essential steady self through it all can be helpful for the meditator to remain calm and centred amidst the fluctuations of thoughts, emotions and sensations within the practice. The sense of inner stability and non-reactive awareness cultivated through the practice of the mountain meditation can then be extended to external difficult circumstances or uncontrollable events in daily life outside of the formal practice. Like weather patterns and seasons, life's challenges can vary in nature and impact but inevitably come and go too and we can be more like the mountain in approaching them and not allowing them to "get in on us".

## Letting Go of Expectations of Others

The acknowledgement that we have choice and agency about how we choose to approach situations and interact with people in our lives is key to attaining a life of more ease and peace. When we choose to judge people, we are creating unnecessary suffering in a similar way. Neil Strauss said, "unspoken expectations are premeditated resentments." We sometimes load OUR expectations onto others in terms of how they should behave and when they don't act in the manner we expect, we become disappointed, frustrated and angry. Unless there is some kind of contract or communicated agreement in place, the other party may not be even aware of the expectations we are placing on them and we expect some sort of mind reading to take place. We mistakenly assume our norms and standards are shared by everyone but like we explored in chapter 2, everyone has a very unique way of seeing and processing life based on their exclusive combination of life experiences.

A simple example I noticed in myself recently, was when I went to meet someone for coffee. They kept their phone on the table for the duration of the meeting, which I judged as impolite. Each time it would beep, they would impulsively check it or just at random intervals, unconsciously pick it up for a look at the screen, which I felt was disrespectful. With some moments of presence, I noticed the associated energies I was feeling in my body, like clenching in my jaw, furrowing in my forehead and contracting in my chest. I went through my internal process of naming the emotions; frustration and annoyance and simply acknowledging them and investigating how they were arising in my body, including temperature, shape and size and then taking care of them by directing some calming breaths into the areas. After that, I had the steadiness to realise that the actions of the person had nothing to do with me, it was not for me to take personally, this was simply their norm of behaviour, their habitual pattern and they were not intentionally being impolite or disrespectful. MY feelings were entirely on me. From this place of insight and awareness, I was able to re-set and I placed my attention without the distraction of self-made emotions back fully onto the conversation. I was even able to muster an attitude of gratitude for the opportunity to enjoy a coffee with a friend and without any expectations, simply savour the moment. Just because they didn't align with MY expectations, it didn't make them wrong or bad in any way. It just was what it was…and it was up to me to manage myself in it. If my intention is to live my life with peace and ease, then I take action towards that no matter what the circumstances are around me.

As a society in general, we can act in a very entitled way at times. For example, we always seem to be angry with the government but we forget that we must take some responsibility too. We voted them into these positions and we delegated authority to them to make decisions on our behalf. That's what we have agreed, that's the contractual arrangement! If they are making decisions that are not in alignment to what they said they would do throughout the campaigning process, well yes, for sure we are within our rights to contact the local representatives to call this out and voice our concerns. But having worked under micro-managing bosses in the past, the work is made so much more difficult when you have a job to do and there is someone looking over your shoulder constantly pointing out how you are not doing it as they think you should. So maybe offering OUR elected representatives our trust and allowing them the space to get on with the job without having to deal with our ongoing complaints might be a win-win for everyone! (Just an idea!). I also think that until a day ever comes that I am prepared to run for elections and do the work of an elected representative myself, I am happy to vote and then let the representatives do what they do best, which frees up my energy to do what I do best. I am not saying that there isn't a place for peaceful protest and demonstration when there is something seriously at odds to our core beliefs, this is absolutely essential at times. But what I am getting at is the level of negative, destructive emotion and rhetoric that goes along with some daily mundane issues – it just seems that some people can get hooked, like addicts, on the adrenaline of protesting against the system, and they seem to jump from one issue to the next to get the opportunity to feel a buzz of anger and frustration with the world. I suspect, if they were brave enough to give themselves the time and space to look inwards, it is actually pain within themselves that is the real source of the anger. Just like the storytime in the previous chapter, the world is our reflection. But just as I experienced in the past, it is a lot easier to distract and point the finger at someone else to avoid the hard work of introspection.

## Already Complete

We can load OUR expectations onto romantic partners too. Thinking they should make us feel attractive, loved, happy etc. but unless we have these feelings towards ourselves, what another person can offer is, at best, a temporary buzz of reassurance and pleasure relative to a long lasting internal contentment, confidence and fulfilment, which can only be self-cultivated. Growing up I often heard the, "I'll be happy when I've a partner" attitude where people attach themselves to the belief that if a certain person, or maybe even a yet unknown suitor, is not in their lives then it is impossible for them to be happy. The truth is, of course, that another person cannot make you truly and sustainably happy and fulfilled - that's an inside job. We want a partner to give us unconditional love while we have a list of conditions for them. Look at a dating app and you will see people's lists of requirements, from height to implied bank balances. First dates become a box checking exercise as opposed to an opportunity to be fully present and enjoy a moment. Instead of allowing the person to be who they are and savor the moments with them in their company, we begin the assessment process and judge them out of our lives based on how we think they should be or how we think they will be in the future. I'm not saying there's any harm in having a few non-negotiables in terms of traits for a person that we will like to spend significant time with but it's when the prerequisites become extreme that we are setting ourselves up for disappointment and suffering. It is unrealistic to believe that one person can be everything to us, that's why we have community, with everyone playing to their strengths ideally. Love or whatever else we are seeking must be nurtured in ourselves first or we will continue to feel lack and continue to mis-place the blame on someone or something outside of ourselves, thinking that they need to fill our gaps. We need to take the responsibility of filling our own cup!

After decades of never feeling good enough, I've happened across another realisation through mindfulness introspection recently and that is the fact that we all have what we need within us to achieve happiness and fulfillment. Despite what society and that awful "you complete me" quote in the film "Jerry Maguire" might suggest, we do not need anything outside of ourselves to be complete and whole. Yes, social connection and community are really important to our well-being and from my own experience, I believe that if we are well connected to our bodies and minds, taking care of ourselves and living authentically, we will attract these connections into our lives without effort. However, growing up, as a young woman in Ireland at least, there was a real sense of urgency once you were in your twenties to "find a man". "Any man with you?", "have you found a man yet?" or "why don't you have a man, are you too fussy?" were as common as conversations about the weather in everyday life. When I take a look at these sentences now I just think how absolutely crazy they are and how they blatantly instill a sense of lack into a young mind! The underlying assumption was that if you hadn't a partner, there was something wrong with you or you'd failed in some way.

I suppose in a strong Catholic Church culture, it was assumed that you wanted to marry and have children. And again, from direct experience, I know that if you didn't have this deep desire, you were judged as some kind of selfish uncaring type. For various reasons, I'm glad I didn't have children despite the societal pressures and expectations. I believe it's just not for some people. I think a marriage with the view towards taking on the project that is raising children, while highly admirable, is often taken too lightly in society. It sometimes seems that more time, thought, and planning goes into wedding day celebrations and house building plans than goes into the detailed design of how children will be reared. I wonder how often the roles and responsibilities of parents are discussed (and more importantly agreed upon) before the baby making process?! Or are these the "premeditated resentments" left to be dealt with in the future?!

Having experienced some lovely times in relationships and also many great periods of being on my own, the truth for me is that happiness and contentment only exists when I generate it for myself internally first. Yes, it's nice to have someone around at times but it's equally nice to be in my own company too. I can feel equally complete, whole and fulfilled in both scenarios because it is an internal condition, not reliant on anyone or anything externally to me. I can enjoy moments or short periods of time with people, a smile to a passer-by, a pleasant chat with the barista or a conversation with the handsome stranger in the supermarket, without the need for anything more, just enjoying a moment and letting that be enough in itself. Similarly, having a romantic relationship can enhance my life at times. But being careful not to layer on the strain of old inherited expectations that it needs to be in a certain way or for the rest of my life. Instead just enjoying the time by being fully present has been so valuable.

## From Burnout to Bliss

We can throw away so many opportunities to share our joy and memorable moments by busying ourselves in the futile exercise of trying to predict where it will all end up and fixating on the future while we are missing the bliss of the present.

I have often blindly applied my financial work mode on my personal life. I have done many a cost/benefit forecast on a potential partner and found the ROI (return on investment) didn't stack to where I thought it should be, then throw the babe out with the bath water so to speak. Nowadays I leave the spreadsheets down and just turn to setting my intention to enjoying moment by moment without needing it to be anything other than what it is. I take the "walk of life" view and set my intention to enjoying the company of and possibly learning and growing with this walking companion for a while, for however long I'm destined to join them on the path. Relationships are great vehicles for accelerating learning about ourselves. If you can remain, present, open and aware, they highlight areas for your further progression towards healing and growth.

Equally though, it is worth mentioning at this point, that the person often referred to as the "happiest man in the world" is Matthieu Ricard, a French Tibetan Buddhist monk, author, and photographer. He attributes his happiness to practices such as meditation, altruism, and compassion and emphasises the importance of inner development and mental training. The title is attributed to him on the basis of neuroscientists having found through fMRI scans of the brain, exceptionally high levels of activity in the area of the brain associated with positive emotions and a reduced propensity towards negative emotions. All that to say, that the happiest man in the world is single! Just sayin'…Ha! Ha! ☺

Eilis O'Grady

## Flying Solo

For a long time I bought into the societal attitude and believed that some knight in shining armour was going to arrive into my life someday to save me and we would "live happily ever after"… another horrendously damaging conditioning from children's fairy tale books. With the internal work through counselling, mindfulness and life coaching, I realised that there was no one coming to save me, neither was there anyone to blame for how my life was unfolding, I needed to take responsibility for my life myself and make the necessary changes towards what I wanted. Through lived experience, I believe now that everyone has potential to grow, change and mould their behaviour, habits and ultimately their lives in whatever way they choose and at any stage in life. There are no limits to our capabilities except those we hold in our minds.

In early April 2024, having booked an Air BnB for a month initially, I arrived in Spain with the intention of really just taking some time out alone to pause and reflect on the past year or two, particularly in terms of the career change out of corporate and into mindfulness. I wanted to just let the dust (or as I like to say in yoga class, the snow globe) settle and just check in with myself and where things were at. I didn't know anybody living in Spain, I didn't know the language, and it was just me in my own company. Mindfulness practice has taught me that calm brings clarity and so I set out to create some calm. After extending my stay a further 2 months in the Air BnB, I finally decided to sign an 11 month contract for a longer term rental apartment on the Costa del Sol.

Still on my own, still not speaking Spanish. As I relayed my plans to people, I was generally met with one of two types of reactions (1) the "you must be having a great time drinking Sangria by the pool every day" or (2) the more caring "are you not lonely by yourself over there?".

First off, I didn't dip in a pool or the sea for 3 months although I did sit on the beach to meditate a lot! And the last drink I had had was a Bailey's with my Mam at the fire on the night before I left for Spain. I think not drinking while alone and settling in here has been one of the things I am most proud of, especially with it being so freely available at any hour or in any coffee shop. It reflects a huge change in me over the past few years. As anyone who knows me for a long time could attest, I was fairly "fond of the drink". Fairly typical, no doubt… living for the weekends for boozy nights out and medicating with glasses of wine for stress relief outside of that. At the time, I saw nothing wrong with it, knowing that many other people around me were doing much the same!

But looking back now, and having equipped myself with a mindfulness based introspection tool kit, I understand that drinking, for me, was an avoidance of feelings strategy. In my drinking days, there were always people around, packed pubs and plenty of social boozy events to choose from. Ironically, I felt more loneliness in these crowds than I have ever felt living on my own. Back then, I was afraid to look at myself, I hated what I saw at the surface, never mind going any further! But through mindfulness based work, I have built trust and a really good relationship with myself. I like my own company now. I believe that the source of loneliness is disconnection from myself, for example, when what I'm doing and saying are misaligned, or when my physical, emotional and mental fuel tank is depleted from not taking care of myself. When I did things and went places just to please others or to keep in with societal norms at the expense of what I really wanted, it wiped out my energy leaving me feeling exhausted. Betraying myself bred resentment, ill health and negative energy in the long run.

When I'm disconnected with myself, it is impossible to connect deeply with others. I just cannot give to another what I don't have for myself and the result is loneliness. So no, I'm not drinking Sangria in Spain and I'm delighted to say that I'm definitely not drinking to mask any loneliness – because I don't feel lonely! Meditation keeps me aligned and connected with myself, which affords me the energy and capacity to make wise choices for myself and enjoy making connections with others who are meeting with the real me. Yes, there are definitely less quantity of people around since I've dropped the drink and the people-pleasing but the quality of connections has enhanced significantly. People living in the safe survival mode don't like others changing around them because it creates a sense of losing control and they prefer if everyone just stays in their assigned boxes. (Remember the "stay down, stay quiet and no one gets hurt" emergency type approach from chapter 6). However, since I took the decisive action and broke out of my box, significantly more genuine connections, clarity and calm has emerged in my life.

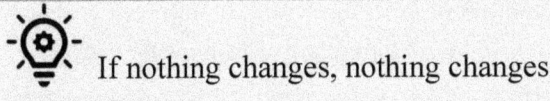 If nothing changes, nothing changes!

## Being at Home in Myself

The whole Spanish adventure also brought me to reflect on the concept of "being at home". The term immediately conjures up feelings of warmth, peace and ease. It's a loaded phrase, with maybe slightly varying meanings for everyone, but in general, covers things like a sense of security, safety, comfort, relaxation and belonging. So how then, is it possible to hop on a plane destined far from "home" to a place I've never been before, not know anyone there, not even know the language and yet, despite all that feel "at home". We often call our house our home but I imagine (and I am grateful that I can only imagine) that if that house was a place filled with turmoil, constant negativity or, worse, domestic abuse that it wouldn't feel much like "being at home". So I conclude then that it's not a physical place and instead is something internal. I have found that "being at home" is felt when my body, heart, mind and actions are connected and aligned with each other…living yoga. Just like building and maintaining a house, an internal home is an ongoing project with regular upkeep and improvement activities necessary. As I have said many times before, this comes through making regular visits to the internal dwelling and checking in by way of practices such as meditation, yoga and journaling. "Being at home" is more about being comfortable with and connected to the authentic and real me and living my life accordingly, which may be in a way that no one else understands or comprehends ... and that's absolutely ok. My life does not have to make sense to anyone else.

A sense of worthiness and value needs to be self-generated, an inside-out approach. It's garnered through the practice of looking inwards, doing the inner work, and resourcing myself. It's about having the skills and capacity to develop qualities internally so that they can be shared readily to those around me. For example, as noted in the discussion of the Loving Kindness practice, if I want to love and be kind to people, it's essential that I cultivate those virtues towards myself first. I replenish the well through practice - formally through meditation and/or informally, through talking to myself like a good friend or even maybe spraying on the Chanel No.5 for a ZOOM call, which makes me smile every time... "'cos I'm worth it" as the saying goes! In contrast, the outside-in approach involves depending on outside sources for my sense of self- esteem. It stems from a sense of lack, of not feeling good enough and relying on external validation to feel good about myself. Being the good girl, the conscientious employee or striving to be skinny were all past ways of obtaining approval from authority, family and society. What may have looked like kind and generous behaviour to others was really just a scream for attention, acceptance and external approval. Aesthetically, the results of acts of kindness from both approaches may look similar but they will feel very different. The outside-in approach carries a sense of neediness, striving for compliments and acknowledgement, like a drug addict seeking the next "hit"- it's exhausting. The inside-out approach, however, is much more relaxed and carefree, with no attachment to the outcome or the receiver's response.

## Ticking the boxes

It's funny what beliefs we take on growing up. As I always say, I can only speak for myself but there are certainly a few myths that I have de-bunked over the last few years for myself. If the following profile was presented to me, at say, 18 years of age, as to how my future was going to look, I think I would have likely fallen into a deeper depression than I was already in at that time. But here it is:

- M/F: Female
- Age: 45
- Marital status: Single
- Children: No
- "Big" House: No
- "Big" Pensionable Job: No
- "Big" Car: No
- "Big" Social Life: No

And yet, without a shadow of a doubt, I am the healthiest and happiest I have ever been in my adult life! Of course, it wasn't always the case that I was as happy with my status. There was a time (not so long ago), and during which time I actually had the house, the car, the pensionable job and the packed social life, where I was striving to get the other boxes ticked to complete the happy-life formula that I'd been implicitly given by society, media and Hollywood ideals. As an example, I remember attending morning management briefings in the factory where we would stand in a semi-circle with our notebooks in hand giving accounts of the latest updates from our respective departments.

I would intentionally position my hands underneath the diary in such a way so that my left hand was covered from view to hide the shame and embarrassment of not having an engagement ring or a wedding ring like everybody else. In more recent years, however, through "my work" in mindfulness, I have come to realise that the original formula was flawed. It was a one size fits all approach, sold to a population of very different shaped and sized human beings. Each individual with a unique set of qualities, preferences, histories, experiences and exclusive blends of physical, mental and emotional components. So I started out with a blank sheet and re-created my own personalized happy life equation and aside from my white summer beach dress, there's no other white dress on my wish list … there's not even a wish list anymore!!

 **Exercise – Consider a typical day in your life:**

**Part 1 – IDENTIFYING**

- Write down how you spend your time
- Beside each activity – note whether you find it a "Nourishing" or "Depleting" or "Mastery" activity.

N = nourishing or nurturing; lifts my mood; gives me energy; increases my sense of being alive

M = mastery; satisfaction once complete; sense of accomplishment or control

D = depleting or draining; dampens my mood

> **Part 2 – RE-BALANCING**
>
> - More regular Nourishing activities?
> - Savour Nourishing activities more and not multitasking?
> - Are there Depleting tasks you could let go of?
> - Could you approach any of the Depleting tasks differently? In a different mode of mind?
> - Could you turn towards the difficult rather than doing the Depleting tasks through gritted teeth, resenting them as a chore or unwanted task?
> - Do you in fact need to make more time for doing any of the Depleting tasks so that you can do them in a different mode rather than in a hurry?

## Mind Yourself

By looking at a typical day, break it down into chunks of activities and beside each activity, note if it is nourishing, depleting or is something we term "mastery". The latter are things that give a sense of accomplishment, satisfaction, or control when they are complete, while they may not be particularly pleasurable in themselves, but something in the world is different after doing them. Nourishing and depleting activities are determined by whether or not they lift the mood, give energy, nourish, or increase the sense of being alive.

The activity invites us to become more intentional around our precious time and energy investments and ultimately our lives. If things appear off balance, then it might be time to "balance the books" by crediting your energy account with nourishing activities such as a walk in nature, a creative activity, gardening, listening to music, etc. Personally, I save a list of nourishing activities on my phone and if I feel a low mood is coming on, I go to the list for ideas and prescribe myself something from it…a much healthier method of self-medicating than what I used to engage in previously. I know from experience that when energy is dipping, the thought of "I don't feel like it" will likely arise. By acknowledging this and getting into the practice of over-riding that thought, I tend to choose better more frequently and take a walk or whatever the "medicine" is. When I do, I end up feeling more energised and happy only 100% of the time!

The habit of a strong morning routine is something else that I introduced early in this journey towards re-discovering myself. The combination of elements within how I spend the first hour (or two) of my day may change over time but the reverence I have for building solid foundations for the day is steadfast. Elements have or do include yoga, meditation, journaling, sea swimming or walking…and a lovely mindful coffee of course. For others I know, reading, breathwork, grounding bare feet onto the earth and going to the gym are more their thing. I try to include something for body, heart and mind. Affirmations are another option; positive, empowering statements that are repeated to oneself to cultivate a more optimistic mindset and reinforce desired beliefs or behaviours. They can prove not only helpful in programming positivity into the mind for the day ahead but can also be used as a meditation technique to focus the attention away from future and past thinking throughout the day. See some examples below.

Whatever your chosen combination for a morning routine, it is a powerful way to start the day and without doubt will have a lasting impact for the entire day.

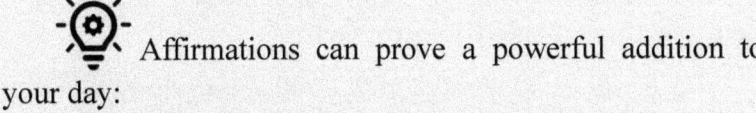 Affirmations can prove a powerful addition to your day:
- Use the present tense.
- Short phrases work best.
- Even if you don't really believe what you are saying is true yet, or it feels awkward, say it anyway. Say it as if you already have whatever it is you want or want to feel.
- Repetition will program the mind into believing it and will seek ways to prove it's true.

*Examples:*

✓ *I am happy, I am healthy and I love my life*
✓ *I have so much abundance in my life*
✓ *I am attracting ...[love, money, relationships] ... into my life*
✓ *I am feeling calm, peace and ease*
✓ *I can achieve anything I set my mind to*

**Storytime… Copying from Copies**

A new young monk arrives at a monastery and he's assigned to help the other monks and copy the old cannons and laws by hand.

But he notices that all of the monks are grimly working in their own cubicles and they're copying from copies … not the original manuscript.

So the new monk goes to the Abbott to question this. He points out that if somebody made a small error in the first copy it wouldn't be picked up. In fact it would be continued in all subsequent copies.

The Abbott says "well we have been copying from copies with centuries but you make a good point my son".

So the Abbott goes down into the dark caves under the monastery where the original manuscripts were being held, in a locked vault, which hasn't been opened for hundreds of years.

Hours go by and nobody sees the old Abbot so eventually the young monk gets worried and goes downstairs to look for him. He sees the Abbott banging his head against the wall and crying uncontrollably. The young monk says "father, father what's wrong?" and in a choking voice the old Abbott replies, "the word is CELEBRATE, not celebate!"

The danger of doing what's always been done. Stay curious. Keep connecting with intention. Keep growing. Be You.

**Pause, Breathe, Reflect**

- Are there areas in your life that you are blindly following the crowd and taking on the societal norms without asking if they are truly serving you?
- If nothing changes, nothing changes. What aspects of your life would you like to improve? What's stopping you?

# CHAPTER 8 – THE JOURNEY AHEAD

*"Make sure you weave your parachute every day, rather than leave it to the time you have to jump out of the plane." — Jon Kabat-Zinn*

Jon Kabat Zinn talks about incorporating mindfulness practice into your life daily and it being akin to weaving and maintaining your parachute so that on the days that you will need it most, it will be available and strong enough to hold and support you.

**If in doubt, meditate…**

Mindfulness practice is all about learning how to face whatever comes up in your life by pausing, taking a wide perspective, and then choosing wisely while taking care of yourself. While we can't control everything that arises in life, we can certainly move and show up in an intentional and mindful way in furtherance to a fulfilling life. In so far as we can be sure, we only get one chance at this and it is up to each of us to become at least a co-creator in it. The previous exercise in chapter 7 "Nourishing and Depleting Activities" not only shows us how to resource and take good care of ourselves but also serves to bring into sharp focus how we spend our life's time. And as the saying goes, how we spend our days is how we spend our lives. Suffice to say, I find it imperative to regularly review how I am spending my valuable time, knowing the moments turn to hours, hours to days and days into the life I will someday look back on with either a full heart of joy or a deep, heavy regret. There's a real danger of just repeating days, years and decades out of fear of not making changes and life becomes bland, colourless and life-less. Regularly taking stock of how days are generally spent is crucial to avoid this happening. Asking whether these daily activities are aligned with what's most important to me in my life; in alignment to my purpose. Caring less about how my life looks and more about how it feels and is experienced, i.e. with frustration and busyness or with more calm, peace, joy and ease. Regularly reviewing the daily routines, habits and the narratives that might be keeping the routines in place is essential to ensure that what I am engaged with is in service to a full and happy life. If not, bravely adjusting as necessary.

As we looked at in chapter 1, when we find ourselves stuck in some way, there can be real value in seeking an objective, unbiased professional support of someone like a Coach or Therapist outside of a circle of family and friends. Those who are too close to us can sometimes hold opinions, or beliefs that reinforce your own views and blind spots as opposed to exposing us to more diverse perspectives. An independent sounding board can call us out on the excuses and stories that may be just under our level of awareness. But above all else... meditate. Even for smaller everyday decisions, where I am unsure what action to take next, my mantra is "if in doubt, meditate". I know if I sit and get quiet, the answer is more likely to come. I remember hearing this a number of years ago now and being very sceptical so I understand if you feel the same on reading it here. All I would suggest is to try it out for yourself. When we pause even for a few minutes, there's more clarity, like a still lake, you can see what's in there. You can also hear the wisdom that is naturally inherent in you, as if opening up the space for the heart and gut to have their say and not letting the mind run the show completely. So the full boardroom of the body get to vote on the decision to hand, a more democratic process over the more dictatorship type of ruling that we allow the mind to engage in at times. The rule of thumb I use is, the bigger the decision, the more quiet I get. A retreat for periods of days or weeks can be hugely beneficial when we come to the various crossroads in the path of life.

> 💡 Meditation practice is like washing your teeth – better to do it for a few minutes each day than an hour on Sunday! ☺

## "Your One Wild and Precious Life"

In December 2021, the Christmas before my good friend Pat passed away, she gifted me a book by Maureen Gaffney called "Your One Wild and Precious Life". The title comes from the last line of a Mary Oliver poem called "The Summer Day", which ironically, I now read to my MBSR participants on Week 1 of the course. I love this quote because there is a real sense of empowerment from it and like a wise boss (thank you Matt) said to me one time, with great power comes great responsibility…the responsibility to live in accordance with what's most important to you. But what is it we want to do? This is a big question and again needs to be given time and space to be reflected on. Meditation is where to start. As mentioned, coming into stillness allows you access to the whole of you, the deepest parts of you and not just taking the surface thoughts of the mind. In approaching this broad question, I supplemented my reflection with a type of visualisation technique to create a vision board of what I wanted my life to 1 feel like. I now take coaching clients through this process quite frequently, whereby we create a calm, steady space and then I invite the client to imagine themselves at a point in the future living their fullest lives. Like meditation practice, not so much thinking about what they are doing but more sensing into how they are feeling in their bodies, what they are seeing, saying and hearing. They don't need to know what exactly makes them feel like this in terms of what activities or jobs they are engaged in, they are just invited to visualise how they would like to feel if they were living their happiest lives imaginable. They don't need to know how it is going to happen, they just sense and feel into what we call the "desired state". Prompts include phrases like:

- I feel …
- My body is feeling…
- I am …
- I have …
- I am enjoying …
- I see myself …
- I am hearing myself say…

- I hear people saying:
- My first thoughts in the morning are:
- My last thoughts at night are:

The resulting description is noted, reflected back to the client for any omissions or adjustments necessary and written up in the present tense. It is important to use the present tense and also to use positive statements. For example, instead of maybe saying, "I am not stressed", use "I am calm" or instead of "I am not sick", say "I am healthy". The mind clings to the descriptor word more than the negative before it. (It's like the classic example of "don't think of a red bus!"). Depending on how the person learns best, be it auditory or visual, this description might be read and voice recorded or it might be translated into a vision board format. Whatever way is chosen the client is encouraged to either read, listen to or picture this desired state of being on a daily basis as a way of programming it into the brain. If it is depicted by way of a vision board, placing it somewhere where it can be seen every day is best. I made several revisions of vision boards over the years and found them to be so powerful. I would open up a blank sheet on Microsoft Word or PowerPoint and then search for images via Google that represented my desired state. I would use some type of snip app to cut and paste onto the blank sheet and make a collage representing what was important to me in all areas of my life…showing love, life and laughter etc. Making the picture as big, bold, and colourful as you would like your life to be, not shying away from anything that your mind might judge as "far-fetched" or "aspirational". Remembering not to allow the dictatorship of the mind to take over this project is key!

## Finding the Path of Passions and Purpose

After you have absorbed the sense of being that you want to cultivate more of, the next question will often be, "but what do I love?" My first port of call would be to start reflecting on my past, more specifically my early childhood memories. This period of life can hold valuable clues because it's the time before so many protective layers of learned and conditioned behaviours were securely fastened over your true nature. It's a time when we weren't hiding behind so many masks, disguises and identities to feel safe in the world. We were more carefree, more real. Later in life, when we get caught up in busyness, titles, roles and ticking boxes, from getting school exams, to getting to college, to securing the "good job", to finding a partner, to building the house, to having the children etc., it's no wonder that we end up forgetting what we love to do. There's just no space and time made for our creative passions and play in most cases. Yet it's important to remember what our strengths are and what we love to do if we want to re-discover more joy in life.

I have found that reflecting on my childhood memories has been a very insightful exercise. Asking what memories stick out as being particularly enjoyable and fun? These are where the clues lie to answering what you love and are particularly good at. Those activities you engaged in before you started layering on the protective covers of psychological protection. Those things that make your heart sing.

When I was about four, we moved to live in Broemountain, where I grew up in the stunningly green wilds of rural West

## Eilis O'Grady

Waterford, surrounded by nature and opportunities for childhood adventures around the hills and woodlands. My Mam tells the story that on the first day I woke up in Broe, I looked out the window and said "look at all the lovely flowers Mammy!" referring to the yellow furze bushes that the house was surrounded by at the time, having been built on the side of a mountain. Mam and others found this hilarious because to all the farming community, of course, furze were invasive weeds and had a very negative connotation in terms of quality of land. But I like this story because I think there is a clue in this story for me as to *my* true nature of seeing the positive, which for many years, I had forgotten. Like most of us, the busyness of ticking boxes through life creeps in, we don the uniform, tow the line and we start to forget so much about our unique qualities, our true essence and our real selves. I recognise that being able to see beauty within the thorns of life is a strength that serves me well in my work as a life coach, seeing the potential beneath the current, unhappy state.

In secondary school, I loved art and essay writing. I remember the cover of my sketch pad and the joy in opening a clean new page of my copy book to put pen to paper. However, these creative pursuits took time and an art portfolio for the Leaving Cert was a huge commitment relative to the more attainable exam points that one could attain from say, Home Economics. "Anyway, sure you couldn't earn money doing art!" was the general sentiment of the time. So the subjects and college course choices were filtered through these anti-creativity lenses', and being very squeamish when it came to blood and veins ruled me out in any health related profession such as nursing or medicine. I landed on a broad generic business studies course in UL with German because "you had to have a language" as the ECC / EU was becoming an increasingly important institution for Ireland. That's what led me to accounting and as I said, to a point, it worked fine for many years. But long term betrayal of myself and too much time away from engaging in activities that I loved and that gave me energy took its inevitable toll.

Another example was remembering what my favourite toy was as a child, which without hesitation, was the navy blue and white Petit 990 typewriter. I loved the click of the buttons and the sound of the scroll being pushed back to form a new row – just like in the opening credits of Jessica Fletcher's "Murder She Wrote" TV series at the time if anyone remembers! By virtue of the fact that you are now reading my recollections, serve to illustrate how I am reclaiming my love for clicking words out, albeit from a computer keyboard these days. Another vivid memory was the thrill I got from hanging from my waist across the side cross bar of the set of swings we had at home in the garden. I loved the sensation of being upside down and with the assistance of my yoga teacher training in recent years, I reignited a regular practice of headstands and other inversions since I turned forty, which I absolutely love. There are many other memories that have guided me to exploring activities that I now find fulfilling and uplifting.

### Questions to get started with:

- What did you love to do as a child?
- What were you naturally good at?
- What energises you and makes you feel alive?
- In what activities do you lose track of time and find flow in?
- What is it that you love to do that positively impacts on others?

Later in my change process, I came across the notion of Ikigai, which guided me towards more specifics around work and how I wanted to spend my time and life. Ikigai, a Japanese concept, translates to "a reason for being" and embodies the idea of finding one's life purpose. It posits that if you can find that thing which (1) you love, (2) you are good at, (3) the world needs, and (4) you can be paid for, then you've likely found your purpose in life. By identifying your ikigai, you align your passions, talents, and values with a meaningful way of life, focusing on what truly matters, ultimately leading to a more balanced and purposeful existence. As humans we change so acknowledging that our purpose can change too is important to note.

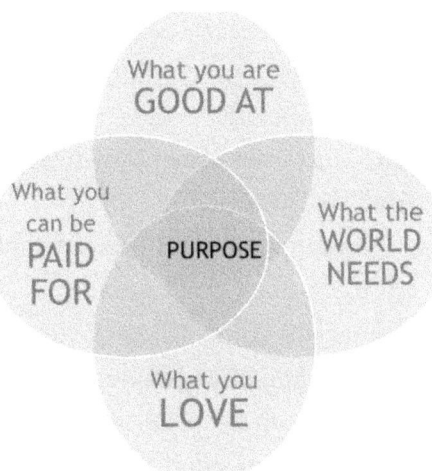

## Prioritise and Pursue – No Excuses

"All sounds great but when am I going to have the time to do that? Sounds like such a luxury but you don't realise how busy I am!"... Do these or similar sentiments sound familiar? To which I can only offer... "if not now, when?" There will always be something on the to-do list, always deadlines at work, always housework to be done but spending days on activities that reap a feeling of less than being fully alive, will soon turn into a lifetime of never having lived. It's vital for health and wellbeing to pursue passions and purpose. If not, we can carry on life in a frenzied resentful unproductive rush, emitting that toxic negative energy and blaming the world for being unfulfilled and unhappy. Be alert for the excuses and old narratives being played by the mind. I often come across people claiming to have no time to take action on their goals, engage in healthy habits or meditate but yet if I asked them what the latest gruesome news headline, celebrity (or local) gossip or viral TikTok was, it would be on the tip of their tongue. It can be a question of priorities. Set your passion and purpose as your priority and let go of the rest.

Granted that being intentional about placing your scarce resources of time, energy and attention onto what's important has likely never been so difficult with the innumerable distractions available at your fingertips via smartphones, yet never so vitally important.

As a way of attempting to illustrate the vast and unprecedented amount of information and news produced these days, thanks to the internet, social media, and 24/7 news cycles, it is said that we can take in more information in one day now than previous generations took in over a lifetime. The consumption of which far exceeds our cognitive limits and beyond the level humans were ever designed to take in. As we reviewed at the end of chapter 5, it's easy to become overwhelmed by it all if we expect ourselves to keep up to date. Yet, as a society, we feel "less than" if we don't know the latest… news or gossip. It's a way of seeking external validation and a sign of low self-worth, we seem to need to be the first to know and being "in the know" has some sort of social one-upmanship attached to it. It takes vast amounts of energy and time scrolling through social media, following the hour by hour news feeds and rarely asking questions like:

- Is this investment of time and energy a wise choice for me?

- Is it aligned to my desired state?
- What quality of energy am I consuming as I take this in? What type of energy is being emitted in my reactions to it?
- Could my time be better spent on either identifying or investing in what's important to me?

These same questions could be applied to any investment of time and energy that we engage in, be it watching TV/Netflix, going to social events, games, or concerts because "everyone" else is going (and we have the FOMO; fear of missing out) or working in a job because that's we have always done. When we are not aware of ourselves we can blindly take on the standardised behaviours from modern society too from unconsciously absorbing through the likes of social media and the news. These can easily become our norms and ways of showing up in the world with our expectations set in reference to them too.

> 💡 Ask yourself regularly – is what I am engaged in aligned to the pursuit of my passions, purpose and vision for my life?

## There is nothing to be feared, only understood...

Fear, fear of change, fear of missing out, or fear of what others think can be strong forces for holding us into an annual life cycle that we repeat for 80 odd years, reliving the same types of experiences, encountering the same types of people and wondering "is this it?" The answer is no! It can be so much more if you allow it to be. As I mentioned earlier, I believe everything we do, every choice we make is made out of one of two sources: (1) love and abundance or (2) fear and scarcity. When we move through life with a mindset of love and abundance, life flows and anything is possible.

What I noticed in myself is that growing up, I had learned a way of being in the world, which gave me a sense of safety and security. I found ways to protect myself, keep myself safe and in control by giving myself identities and putting myself in boxes. If you recall from chapter 2 how I narrated my story to the Counsellor, that I was resigned to having depression for the rest of my life and I had assigned various labels to myself within my box such as "good girl", "diligent", "hard working", "prone to depression", "accountant", "been through a lot", "average", "unattractive", "fat", "ugly", and this would form my identity for life. Holding onto identities and labels we assign to ourselves become our limitations, like living in a self-created security box. It feels safer when things don't change because we know what to expect, even if it is uncomfortable, it's familiar. We can be afraid to lose this control and come out of our boxes into the unknown and relinquish the possibility of discovering something better. We can also be afraid of people's reactions to our pursuing our own needs and dreams. When we let go of people pleasing behaviours, be that of friends or family, they can become uneasy, fearful or even angry with our new choices. And out of fear, they may lay on the guilt trip, labelling us as selfish. Change is not always easy but is worth it. If nothing changes, nothing changes.

Since I began teaching yoga, I've had a couple of classes where no one turned up. And I can proudly say that I rarely took it personally because in recent years, I have come to realise that no experience is ever wasted, there is always something to be learned. Sometimes a reinforced learning, or a reminder I need a rest or sometimes a re-direction back onto the "right path" for where I'm going. In the past, even the thought of arranging a class, never mind having no one turn up to it would have crippled me with anxiety. I wouldn't have allowed myself to get into the situation in the first place; no class would have been created FOR FEAR of nobody showing up. But what was the fear? Fear is a temporary energy moving around in the body, which for me, usually manifests as an unpleasantness in my stomach. And if I don't start adding negative thoughts to create compounding sensations of fear, this biological sensation will dissolve in 90 seconds!! Yes, that's it, 90 seconds! And what if I had let this temporary sensation of fear overpower me? What if I had chosen to allow fear in the driving seat of my life? Well, I would probably be still sitting unfulfilled at my old job and would never have experienced the joy, the chats, the laughs and friendships that have since come from the 100's of classes that I've had the privilege of running since.

Action builds inner belief. "But I'd be afraid of what people would think?", "Who does she think she is?!" These statements were such a huge part of my inner dialogue in the past. It's such a paralysing way of thinking. The beauty of mindfulness is that with practice you grow a fearlessness and a self-worth that's no longer dependent on external validation of others. When I let go of this fear, it was a real game changer and it opened up so many opportunities for new experiences. It was like a ball and chain had been unlocked from my ankles and I was free to fly! With a "Just Do It" approach and taking imperfect action over the years too, I have come to know that no amount of thinking about, reading about, taking courses about, estimating or surmising will ever compensate for just doing the thing and finding out for real … so I just do the thing! Yes, the first time (or indeed anytime) will never be perfect but it's a lot better than the void from inaction. In the long term, taking action and giving it a go saves a lot of time and energy that would otherwise be given over to unproductive rumination and agonising procrastination. What's the worst that can happen? There were plenty of times where I had a new idea, created the event or put on a class for no one to show up and that's ok! I simply take the learnings without any needless judgement or criticism. I actually congratulate myself on giving it a go and almost get excited to know in what direction I am being re-directed to. Like the universe is just telling me – eh eh, wrong turn, reverse, back up, take the other road at the last intersection. Life's an adventure, take the next best step and trust the process that all will be well.

What I'm going to say next still feels a little uncomfortable because even a year ago I don't think I would have said it out loud, but I'm going to let you in on the secret…

# From Burnout to Bliss

"the Universe has your back!" From all that I have experienced since moving towards what I really want, and living life on my own terms, I am convinced that the world works with you when you follow your heart and what's most authentic to you. Opportunities will come from the most unlikely places when you create the space to allow them in. For example, shortly after I left the corporate job, with no solid plan, I met a girl at a funeral that I hadn't seen in near on 20 years. As I shook her hand in sympathy for her loss, she whispered into my ear, "I hear great things about your yoga, I would love if you could come into my place of work, I will give you a call". She did, and that ended up becoming an assignment for multiple weekly classes in a centre for intellectually disabled people, which I absolutely loved and found so rewarding. I get little signs along the way to indicate that I am making the right decisions too. I would have called them coincidences at the start but there have been so many now that I cannot believe that it's merely coincidence anymore. For example, the day I heard about the Masters in Mindfulness was what would have been Dad's 74th birthday; the date of the letter sent to me from the Chartered Accountants of Ireland to advise they had accepted my resignation was 12$^{th}$ Sept 2023… the exact date of my 45$^{th}$ birthday; I left for Spain on 5$^{th}$ April 2024, not realising that I had booked the flights on the anniversary of my good friend Patricia Horan and to add to that, on the day she passed away in 2022, my house sold in Abbeyside. No matter what you call them, I find them of great comfort along the way that something larger than me is at work WITH me. The only proof is that I am living a life that I could only have dreamt about 5 years ago!

Eilis O'Grady

## Time for a Change?

On 15th June 2023, I was due back to the office after a nine month career break that I had taken to complete my Masters in Mindfulness Based Wellbeing in UCC. I was due back to the desk, back to the spreadsheets, back to the daily commute, the emails, the reports, the back to back meetings, the month ends, the audits and the whole daily routine of the financial analyst in a multi-national company… which, as I always say, served me very well for many years, but I felt my heart wasn't in it anymore. And that's ok! Humans evolve, all beings grow, life changes. Just like any long term relationship that has run its course…it was great, exciting and rewarding for a long time but now it was time to leave and I had felt it in my bones for a while.

Long story, short…I never went back after the career break. A highly risky manoeuvre for anyone, yet alone a conservative accountant type, to leave a "good pensionable job" and to go full time mindfulness and yoga teaching, or full time "woo woo" as some might consider it. I could almost hear people thinking, "she must be absolutely mad" and to those who asked me "but what about the pension?", I recalled how my very good friend (and ex-colleague) had recently passed away at the age of 62…and what about her pension?!! What about the long days that she had put in, working so diligently and conscientiously for her pension, never to see a penny of it. I decided I would take the heartbreaking lesson on board, make the change and take the risk for potentially finding a way of life that I would truly love, that I wouldn't feel the need to "retire" from. It didn't take too long…

# From Burnout to Bliss

As I type, I'm looking out the window onto the Costa del Sol. Blue sky, blue sea and the heat of the summer sun radiating the room. But it's not the location or the external weather that really matters. What has changed most is the internal weather pattern; the peace, calm and ease that comes with spending your life's time (whatever duration remains) on what you truly love. Today, for example, I'm getting ready to run my weekly live online yoga class tonight and I am just after receiving a beautiful heartfelt 5-star rated review for my latest offering of the 8-week Mindfulness Based Stress Reduction course, which I finished on Sunday night last... with an amazing group of individuals.

All of this to say... if you are looking to make a change. If your body, heart and mind are crying out for it... do it! Life is too short to be putting it off to retirement or another un-promised point into the future that may never arrive. NOW is the best time to make the change! Things really have a miraculous way of falling into place if you follow your heart. I know that does sound "woo woo" but it's absolutely based on lived experience. If you would like advice, support or an independent sounding board to get the ball rolling, please feel free to reach out to me.

##  Storytime...The Golden Buddha In You

Our early childhood memories can be strong indicators towards our real and authentic selves, which as we grow older, we cover over with protective habits and behaviours to help us cope better, and for some maybe even survive, in the conditions we find ourselves in. We adapt ourselves to the extent that one day, with some momentary awareness we might realise that the gap between what's being presented as our self to the world and what our true nature is has become so distant that we feel completely lost from ourselves; disconnected and lonely. This is a painful junction to arrive at but if we can gather the strength and courage at this point, we can begin the path of returning to ourselves.

There is a story of a massive clay Buddha statue in Thailand, 17 feet tall that came from around the 13th century and was worshipped for several centuries as the "Terracotta Buddha". In the mid 1950's the authorities decided to shift the Terracotta Buddha to a place several kilometres away to do some repairs to the temple that it was housed in. During the final attempt to lift the statue from its pedestal, the ropes broke and the statue fell hard on the ground. At that moment, some of the plaster coating chipped off and to the surprise of the grief stricken onlookers, who thought that their great icon had been destroyed, they noticed that what had chipped was only an outer layer. The core of the Buddha statue was in fact made of pure gold! What had happened was during a time when Thailand was experiencing foreign invasions and fearing that the invaders would take away the golden image, which was 5.5 tons of solid gold, the worshipers at the time covered the golden image with clay. Thinking that it was only a Terracotta Buddha, the invaders left it untouched.

Just like the clay covering the Buddha, humans often develop protective layers. These layers can be understood in terms of behaviours, beliefs, and habits that we adopt over time. With the gift of awareness, a re-discovery can happen if we are prepared to take time and space to do the work of peeling off the layers to reveal the hidden treasure within, our golden essence.

 **Pause, Breathe, Reflect**

- Can you identify any layers of protection that you may have developed to cope better in the world while growing up?
- Do these layers still serve you or is it time to let them go?
- What is it you will do with your one wild and precious life?

# CHAPTER 9 – BUEN CAMINO!

*"If I could offer you only one tip for the future, sunscreen would be it*

*A long-term benefits of sunscreen have been proved by scientists*

*Whereas the rest of my advice has no basis more reliable*

*Than my own meandering experience, I will dispense this advice now"*

— *"Everybody's Free" Song by Baz Luhrmann*

**Some Essentials for the Journey**

In the spirit of the above, I share the following list of some guiding principles that I remind myself regularly:

## *Living Life*

- Focus on finding your strengths and passions in life. Find clues in your childhood.
- Be your best friend. The quality of your relationships with others and the world are dependent on the quality of the relationship you have with yourself!
- Everyone has some sort of creativity inside of them. Ignore it at your peril.
- Don't be paralysed by perfection. This fear of judgement and criticism leads to inaction and unfulfilled dreams.
- Live for the now, there is no other time to live, there is no other time that's real. The past and future are virtual realities.
- Impermanence - everything that is in the nature of arising has also the nature of passing, this too shall pass.
- The opposite of war isn't peace, its creation. Survive or thrive.
- Create space in your life if you want something new in your life.
- There's little joy to be found in multi-tasking.
- As best you can, try stop passing on intergenerational trauma behaviours.
- Being a victim of your past keeps you far from achieving your dreams of the future.
- You will never be faced with anything more than you can cope with. Believe in yourself.
- Number of followers, friends, level of knowledge, money in the bank or weight on a scales are not measures of self-worth.

## *Choice and Change*

- When you believe that you can change and when awareness is available, the world is your oyster. Self-awareness creates choices and empowerment.
- Change is not linear, so go easy on yourself when you fall into an old familiar pothole, pick yourself up, dust yourself off and begin again.
- Change means letting go to create space for something new. The transition will be uncomfortable but will be worth it all on the other side.
- Connect to your intention, ask "why?" often and align actions to what's really important to you.
- Create time for regular stillness and reflection.
- Check your daily forecast - daily check ins on the internal weather pattern and upcoming emotional weather systems. What is needed? Adjust accordingly.
- Doing nothing is better than being busy doing nothing.
- Consider what energy am I going to bring into the world in both thinking about and taking action on this situation?
- Am I making this decision out of fear/scarcity or love/abundance?
- Stay true to you and your tribe will find you.
- When in doubt, meditate.

## *Difficult Emotions*

- Emotions are processed through being with the body. Going to the head for a solution only increases suffering. Thinking can be an avoidance strategy from a fear of feeling emotion.

- All emotions are a signal to something to be taken care of with kindness and curiosity. Take care of your inner child.
- What am I learning here? Obstacles are opportunities to learn. There is no failings only learnings if you remain open to them.
- When my index finger is pointing the finger of blame or the shortcomings in others, remember that there are three fingers pointing back at myself reminding me to undertake some introspection.
- Move your body when you feel stuck.
- What attitude of mindfulness might be helpful here?
- Not everything needs to be judged as either right/wrong, good/bad…
- Trust. Plans "not working out" or rejections can be seen as protection and/or re-directions. If you miss the bus or flight, sit back, relax and trust that it was not meant for you.
- If I am suffering, what is it that I am attached to? Can I let go?
- Annoyed by or jealous of someone? What is it that they are mirroring back to you? What do you see in them that you recognise in yourself? What are you learning about yourself from this annoyance?
- Will this matter a year from now?
- If there is pain, can I bring kindness?
- "What meaning am I giving to this?", "Can I take a wider view and see from another perspective?", "Is a similar past experience clouding my judgement of this interaction?".
- There is nothing to be feared, only understood.
- Mindful Maths

- Pain + Critical, Negative Thoughts = Suffering
- (Pain +/- Suffering) + Kindness = Compassion
- Facts + Our Interpretations = Our Emotions + Our Reactions
- Event + Resistance = Judgement in the Mind + Contraction in the Body
- Event + Resistance = Suffering
- Life Experience = accumulation of moments = Sensations + Impulses + Thoughts + Emotions

- Gratitude is another word for happiness.
- My mood is my responsibility.

## *Physical*

- Don't wear black in the sun!
- Stretch regularly.
- Breathe through your nose. It avoids the load of over-breathing and the nose is a cleaning filter on your face to stop air borne toxins getting into the body.
- Smile!

## The Camino called Life

### "We're all just walking each other home"

This line has had a huge impact on how I look at life now and especially how I interact with people. I see life like a long pilgrim walk, and for anyone familiar with the Camino de Compostela, that's what I envision. I believe as you walk along the road of life, some people will accompany you for short periods along the way while others nearly always seem to be within sight on the horizon or just tailing behind a little. I've walked beside good friends, then parted to take alternate routes and converged with them years later again along the road. Walking beside people for a short time doesn't mean that their impact on your life will be any less than those who are life-long travelling companions. The briefest of encounters can have the most profound influence on the route you choose to take in life. I wonder what my life would be like now if it weren't for two words, i.e. "mindfulness" and "neuroplasticity" that a counsellor mentioned to me in a session about 10 years ago. Or the day I happened to bump into a friend on the Greenway track on 12th July (my Dad's birthday) 2021, who mentioned a course that she thought I just might be interested in and that I should look it up. Only that it was my deceased father's birthday, I would never have taken it as a potential sign and followed through on her recommendation…it turned out to be the Masters in Mindfulness!

    I remind myself that everyone, despite how they may present on the outside, just wants to feel happy, seen and loved on the inside. Sometimes their methods of going about creating happiness seem completely contradictory and paradoxical but ultimately, I believe every being is searching for health, happiness and ease in life. Hurt people hurt people for sure and I know this from having been that hurt person. But 46 years down the path of life and not knowing the length of the journey yet to come for me, I got to reflecting what, if given the opportunity, I would say to my younger self setting out on the road again. In some ways, I feel I have that opportunity now as I watch my beautiful little niece Nancy and handsome nephew Jack grow in their 5th and 4th years of life respectively. I can see so much of myself in Nancy especially and I would like that this work to be an exploration of what I might say to her over the next years as she grows the capacity to receive the, often times, hard earned, young but steadily growing wisdom of her auntie Eilís. My breakthrough in terms of self-awareness has really only come in recent times as I hit the big four oh (40) in 2018. Over the past 6 years, I often heard myself utter the words – "if I only knew this earlier in life", or "if only they taught this in schools". With that and the fact that there are no guarantees that I will be around to share my story in-person (as we are so frequently reminded) or that my mind will continue to have the ability to remember the lessons of the journey so far, I have decided to get them down on paper. It's far, far from perfect, especially in terms of literacy elegance, but it now exists outside of my mind, which is of far more use than an unactioned thought.

All the academic papers and research information in the world are literally at our fingertips nowadays whenever we want it but what artificial intelligence (AI) can't provide is what parts of the infinite well of data is most helpful and useful to you and how to filter what's most relevant. My intention is that you can be guided by my stories to find the resources that fit your needs. We can be paralysed by choice and overwhelmed at the amount of content available so keeping this book concise and to the point has been intentional so as not to add to that information overload. I would like this work to be enjoyed and taken in as if having a conversation with a fellow adventurer and where seeds of ideas might be planted softly in your vast open awareness to germinate in their own time.

In recalling stories from my past, I attempt to be as accurate as possible but of course details and chronology is often hazy looking back, especially when the stories are so often from a time of internal turmoil. Inbuilt human defences block out memories of unpleasant events, and along with them, the pleasant events as a coping mechanism. So in-keeping with the intention to be succinct, when I speak about phases and longer periods of time in my life, please note that I do so with very broad brush strokes to give the general sense of my prevailing mind states around these times in my past. It's so important for me to reiterate that, even in the darkest of stages, I experienced bright and beautiful people, moments and life events that I will cherish forever.

# A Note on the MBSR

**Mindfulness Based Stress Reduction Course**

My Masters in Mindfulness Based Wellbeing from University College Cork qualifies me to teach the 8 week Mindfulness Based Stress Reduction (MBSR) course and I do so regularly. The MBSR course is an evidence-based programme that was specifically designed for stress management. It offers secular, intensive mindfulness training and since its introduction in the 1970's, has been integrated into Western healthcare not only to cope with stress but also to help alleviate a range of conditions including chronic pain, sleep disorders, depression, anxiety, and burnout. It uses techniques like meditation, breathing and yoga and helps people become more aware of their thoughts and feelings so that, instead of being overwhelmed by them, they are better able to manage them. It is a well-defined educational approach, with an established curriculum designed to teach participants in a group setting how to practice mindfulness meditations, cultivate mindfulness in their daily lives and to take better care of themselves. The intervention involves 2.5 hour sessions on a weekly basis for 8 weeks, consisting of experiential and group exercises and participants are encouraged to complete home meditation practice 6 days a week between weekly sessions. If you have been, are, or considering to be a participant on the 8 week Mindfulness Based Stress Reduction (MBSR) course, I have organised the chapters of this book so that they follow the weekly content structure of the 8 week MBSR curriculum, albeit loosely at times. My intention is that the chapter material might supplement and enhance the learning experience of the course by underpinning the themes through the sharing of my practical lived application (and non-application at times) of the concepts presented each week. Should you wish to participate in one of these courses, please reach out to me.

# WORKING WITH ME

As a valued reader, I hope that this book will serve as a map or travel guide along your own path or a catalyst for more adventure and fun through the camino of life. So thank you... thank you for choosing to read and I hope you find my story helpful in some way.

If you would like to work with me to reduce stress, increase wellbeing and create a life you love, I would be honoured to walk with, listen to and support you in your journey, because at the end of the day, **we are all just walking each other home.**

*Eilís O'Grady*
*Mindfulness, Yoga and Life Coaching*
*+353 87 6523410*
www.eilisogrady.ie
www.instagram.com/eilisogrady
www.facebook.com/eilis.ogrady

Buen Camino!

# Bibliography

Brach, T. (2012). Radical acceptance: Awakening the love that heals fear and shame. Random House.

Kabat-Zinn, J., & Hanh, T. N. (2009). Full catastrophe living: Using the wisdom of your body and mind to face stress, pain, and illness. Delta.

Mayers, C. (2018). How to find your Ikigai and transform your outlook on life and business. Forbes< https://www. forbes.com/sites/chrismyers/2018/02/23/how-to-find-your-ikigai-and-transform-your-outlook-on-life-and-business.

Neff, K. (n.d.). Self-Compassion. https://self-compassion.org/

Salzberg, S. (n.d.). Loving Kindness. https://www.sharonsalzberg.com/

Tolle, E. (2009). A new earth: create a better life. Penguin UK.

# ACKNOWLEDGMENTS

For many years, I was lost from myself and consequently lonely, sad and hurt. As I said, hurt people, hurt people and for those who were hurt as a result of my self-loathing… I AM TRULY SORRY.

To my parents Kit & Jack, sister Elaine and brother Walter who saw me at my lowest and supported me throughout; from the bottom of my heart…THANK YOU.

To my friends, extended family and my previous work colleagues from the corporate world, some of whom I mentioned already, I truly appreciate your friendship, encouragement and guidance through my transition into this new career. Special mention to Cecilia Shefflin, my first mindfulness teacher, who has since become a trusted friend… THANK YOU.

To the beautiful beings who attend/(ed) my classes and courses over the past number of recent years, I can't tell you how wonderful it is to have the opportunity to share space with people who are equally eager to learn and grow… THANK YOU.

To the change makers who, by their brave steps, have inspired and encouraged me on my journey of change and finding my heart path, with a special mention to the beautiful Emer Enright (RIP), who passed on 28th Dec 2024 … THANK YOU.

To the writers who inspired me to transform this brainwave to a book. To Páraig de Búrca for helping me to believe it was possible and to Tasha Lanigan for designing my beautiful butterfly logo… THANK YOU.

And to you the reader…THANK YOU.

Love to you all x
Eilís

www.ingramcontent.com/pod-product-compliance
Lightning Source LLC
Chambersburg PA
CBHW041306110526
44590CB00028B/4266